Careers
for the
Twenty-First
Century

Law

by Sheri Bell-Rehwoldt

LUCENT BOOKS

An imprint of Thomson Gale, a part of The Thomson Corporation

THOMSON

™

GALE

Detroit • New York • San Francisco • San Diego • New Haven, Conn.
Waterville, Maine • London • Munich

For Siobhan, my sister and cheerleader

LIBRARY OF CONGRESS CATALOGING-IN-PUBLICATION DATA

Bell-Rehwoldt, Sheri.
   Law / by Sheri Bell-Rehwoldt.
      p. cm. — (Careers for the twenty-first century)
   Includes bibliographical references and index.
   ISBN 1-59018-401-7 (hardcover : alk. paper)
      1. Law—Vocational guidance—United States. 2. Practice of law—United States.
I. Title. II. Series.
   KF297.B45 2004
   340'.023'73—dc22
                                              2004011842

Printed in the United States of America

Contents

Foreword

Young people in the twenty-first century are faced with a dizzying array of possibilities for careers as they become adults. However, the advances in technology and a world economy in which events in one nation increasingly affect events in other nations have made the job market extremely competitive. Young people entering the job market today must possess a combination of technological knowledge and an understanding of the cultural and socioeconomic factors that affect the working world. Don Tapscott, internationally known author and consultant on the effects of technology in business, government, and society, supports this idea, saying, "Yes, this country needs more technology graduates, as they fuel the digital economy. But . . . we have an equally strong need for those with a broader [humanities] background who can work in tandem with technical specialists, helping create and manage the [workplace] environment." To succeed in this job market young people today must enter it with a certain amount of specialized knowledge, preparation, and practical experience. In addition, they must possess the drive to update their job skills continually to match rapidly occurring technological, economic, and social changes.

Young people entering the twenty-first-century job market must carefully research and plan the education and training they will need to work in their chosen careers. High school graduates can no longer go straight into a job where they can hope to advance to positions of higher pay, better working conditions, and increased responsibility without first entering a training program, trade school, or college. For example, aircraft mechanics must attend schools that offer Federal Aviation Administration–accredited programs. These programs offer a broad-based curriculum that requires students to demonstrate an understanding of the basic principles of flight, aircraft function, and electronics. Students must also master computer technology used for diagnosing problems and show that they can apply what they learn toward routine maintenance and any number of needed repairs. With further education, an aircraft mechanic can gain increasingly specialized licenses that place him or her in the job market for positions of higher pay and greater responsibility.

In addition to technology skills, young people must understand how to communicate and work effectively with colleagues or clients from diverse backgrounds. James Billington, librarian of Congress, asserts that "we do not have a global village, but rather a globe on which there are a whole lot of new villages . . . each trying to get its own place in the world, and anybody who's going to deal with this world is going to have to relate better to more of it." For example, flight attendants are increasingly being expected to know one or more foreign languages in order for them to better serve the needs of international passengers. Electrical engineers collaborating with a sister company in Russia on a project must be aware of cultural differences that could affect communication between the project members and, ultimately, the success of the project.

The Lucent Books Careers for the Twenty-First Century series discusses how these ideas come into play in such competitive career fields as aeronautics, biotechnology, computer technology, engineering, education, law enforcement, and medicine. Each title in the series discusses from five to seven different careers available in the respective field. The series provides a comprehensive view of what it is like to work in a particular job and what it takes to succeed in it. Each chapter encompasses a career's most recent trends in education and training, job responsibilities, the work environment and conditions, special challenges, earnings, and opportunities for advancement. Primary and secondary source quotes enliven the text. Sidebars expand on issues related to each career, including topics such as gender issues in the workplace, personal stories that demonstrate exceptional on-the-job experiences, and the latest technology and its potential for use in a particular career. Every volume includes an "Organizations to Contact" list as well as annotated bibliographies. Books in this series provide readers with pertinent information for deciding on a career and as a launching point for further research.

Introduction

A Society Ruled by Law

American society is ruled by law. This is beneficial to citizens, as these laws guarantee them certain basic rights. In theory, no one is allowed to violate the law or infringe on the rights of others. If they choose to do so, they may find themselves defending their actions in a court of law. It then becomes the court's job to ensure that justice is served. As lawyer David Mullally says, "Individuals or private organizations, whether rich or poor, influential or downtrodden, are subject to court process. And the courts and judges themselves are required to follow established procedures and to reach decisions based not on whim, but on generally accepted principles and sound reasoning."[1]

As straightforward as Mullally's statement may seem, navigating the U.S. legal system is anything but simple. But the system works because of the expertise and dedication of millions of individuals who work in the field of law. These individuals play a critical role in society. Lawyers, for example, see to it that their clients know their rights; judges ensure that the law is correctly and fairly applied. Says Stephen Reinhardt, a judge in the U.S. Court of Appeals:

> Without lawyers dedicated to promoting our emerging liberties, without lawyers willing to fight for the rights of the poor and the disadvantaged, without judges with courage, wisdom, and compassion, we would be locked into a rigid and inflexible mode of legal analysis. . . . This nation will not survive as we know it without a strong and independent judiciary, without a dedicated and public spirited bar.[2]

In addition, paralegals and law librarians support lawyers and judges in collecting facts, while court reporters meticulously capture every word spoken during a trial or deposition. And mediators, who help individuals and companies settle disputes without having to go to court, are increasingly becoming an indispensable part of the legal system.

A career in law offers numerous challenges and rewards. Though the work hours are long and the caseloads often heavy, there can be significant intellectual stimulation, monetary reward, and job satisfaction. Those who find success in law careers are driven, curious, intelligent, and dedicated to playing an important role in the betterment of society. A career in law is an ideal choice for those who enjoy research, writing, stimulating interaction, and, above all, helping to solve people's legal problems.

During trial, a judge makes a point to two lawyers standing before his bench as a court reporter (foreground) records every spoken word.

Chapter 1

Paralegals

Paralegals are increasingly at the forefront in the practice of law. According to paralegal Kimberly Sanger, "When people call the firm, they speak to a paralegal first."[3] Moreover, the paralegal has become the workhorse in many law offices. Steve Albrecht, author of *The Paralegal's Desk Reference*, adds: "Attorneys who work in small, midsize, or large firms must have the knowledge, training, educational background, and professional expertise to attract clients and settle their cases, but the day-to-day 'grind it out' paperwork and client management are usually handled by the paralegal staff."[4]

Paralegals (also called legal assistants) now handle many of the tasks that were previously the responsibility of lawyers. Burdened by ever-increasing caseloads, lawyers delegate tasks that must be done outside the courtroom, such as researching, interviewing witnesses, analyzing material and evidence, and maintaining day-to-day contact with clients. Increasingly, those clients appreciate the costs savings that working with a paralegal affords. While a client might be billed $250 an hour if a lawyer collects evidence or drafts a pleading, the rate may drop to $125 an hour if handled by a paralegal.

Most paralegals work for large law firms. Their responsibilities vary widely, says Albrecht:

> If your firm is heavily involved in trial work, you'll probably spend most of your time in court, filing writs, briefs, and motions or helping the attorneys prepare for court. In other firms you may be asked to offer administrative support and help run the whole office in a smooth and orderly fashion. Some firms hire paralegals strictly to help with legal research. Still others use paralegals mainly in a production role: typing and editing briefs, preparing contracts, wills

and trusts; tracking the billable hours for each case; and managing the filing systems.[5]

Paralegal Barbara Lake describes her daily routine at a large insurance defense firm:

A typical day would begin by checking to see what things I had on the calendar for that day: interrogatories that needed to be answered, a complaint that needed to be filed within the next two weeks, whether we had received medical charts from a client's doctor so that my attorney could begin settlement negotiations, etc. If we were still waiting for interrogatory answers from a client, I might have needed to make phone calls to see what the hang-up was. I have even gone to clients' homes to get their answers for interrogatories. If it looked like we were not going to make the deadline for answers, I'd need to call opposing counsel to arrange for an extension.[6]

However, not all paralegals work for law firms or handle lawsuits. Some work in real estate offices, government offices, schools,

A paralegal researches land records in a Texas courthouse. Researching information is one of the many tasks paralegals handle to help attorneys prepare for court.

banks, insurance agencies, and corporations. Whether drafting contracts, mortgages, or patent applications, they interact with many people while completing their tasks.

Wherever they work, successful paralegals share certain traits. Not only are they dependable and organized, they are ingenious problem solvers who rely heavily on their people skills. In addition, they are able to work independently, are comfortable with evolving technology, and are dedicated to learning new skills.

Training and Standards

Although paralegals cannot be held legally liable in a case, they are expected to maintain the same high ethical standards required of attorneys. In addition, since lawyers accept legal responsibility for their paralegals' work, paralegals need to put forth their best effort—or risk losing their jobs.

Paralegals learn their basic skills through formal classroom training. Most law firms and other organizations hiring paralegals expect candidates to have certification from a paralegal program, preferably one approved by the American Bar Association (ABA). Nancy Slaughter, a paralegal manager at a large law firm, says, "The only people we hire for paralegal positions who don't have a certificate are those who intend to go to law school. Those positions are temporary, lasting only two years."[7]

Approximately 250 schools offer ABA-approved two- and four-year paralegal programs, and many schools offer shorter cer-

A legal team meets to discuss the details of a case. Paralegals are integral to the success of any law firm.

School Topics

Paralegal training programs introduce students to a wide variety of topics. Beyond learning the fundamentals of what paralegals do, students learn about law office management, investigation (including techniques of preserving evidence), litigation (an overview of the court process from the initial client interview to the conclusion of the trial), legal researching and writing (including fact gathering, library research techniques, interviewing, and drafting routine legal correspondence), and introductions to family law, criminal law, property law, and estate planning and probate law. During their last two semesters, students typically round out their studies with one or more internships to gain real-world experience. Internships also help the new paralegals to determine the environment in which they would most like to work.

tification programs for students who already have a bachelor's degree. These certificate programs can typically be completed within a year. Regardless of their length, most training programs include an internship in a private law firm, bank, corporate legal department, or government agency.

Some firms, however, occasionally accept candidates with specific skills learned from on-the-job training and continuing education courses. So an applicant with experience in criminal justice, tax preparation, nursing, or health administration might be hired for a paralegal position by a law firm seeking to build those areas of expertise. In general, however, those without formal specific paralegal training will not get an interview.

Major law firms increasingly prefer to hire paralegals who have earned a bachelor's degree in addition to certification. According to the American Association for Paralegal Education (AAfPE), "Although 'on the job training' remains an important element in developing successful paralegals, the role of higher education and formal paralegal education is increasingly important in the growth of the paralegal profession."[8] The requirement of a bachelor's degree troubles many experienced paralegals who lack one. On an online paralegal chat board, a paralegal asks: "Should [firms] show preference to someone with a four-year degree versus someone with 14 years experience?"[9] How relevant a college degree is to the actual requirements of the job is sometimes beside the point. Some firms simply use the degree to narrow the applicant pool.

A law firm might do this to ensure that they hire only the most committed candidates. Working for a law firm is not easy; law firm paralegals typically work longer hours than paralegals employed by corporate and government offices. As Pat Hart, a legal coordinator, explains, "Our firm requires tremendous hours. When a candidate says, 'Sure, I can work those hours,' I need to be assured he means it. Someone who can convince me he will travel, work long hours, and become a professional legal assistant will get my attention."[10] Slaughter adds that those candidates her firm interviews are also informed of required overtime: "The expected hours for each position are spelled out in the job description. Some of our positions require daily overtime; others do not. It varies from office to office."[11]

To reward their dedication, adds Slaughter, many firms organize their paralegals in a tiered structure. Each tier involves added responsibility, social standing, and financial reward. Legal Assistant I is the entry-level position. Typically, after three years a paralegal may be promoted to Legal Assistant II if he or she has mastered routine tasks, needs only minimal supervision, and has earned a certified legal assistant (CLA) designation. This is a voluntary test, offered by the National Association of Legal Assistants (NALA), that some paralegals choose to take to prove their knowledge and to get more advanced jobs. Paralegals with six or more years of experience qualify for a Legal Assistant III position. At this level they are able to competently draft complex legal documents. They also may supervise others. Paralegals in Senior Legal Assistant or Manager positions may have ten or more years of experience, may be certified as specialists in one area of law, and supervise and delegate projects to other paralegals.

The Ideal Paralegal

Although paralegals cannot offer legal advice, many of the attributes of successful lawyers are shared by successful paralegals.

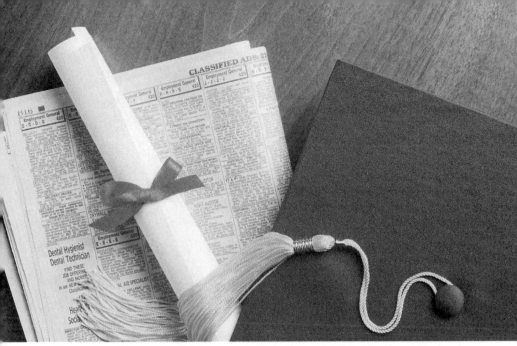

Rewarding jobs are available to graduates of one of the hundreds of paralegal programs approved by the American Bar Association.

These attributes include a high sense of personal responsibility, the ability to juggle tasks by deadline, and reliability: they can be counted on to get the job done. Chere B. Estrin, a trainer and career counselor, describes the ideal paralegal: "When accepting an assignment, the paralegal is accepting responsibility for the project to be completed timely, efficiently, and professionally. Acceptance means agreeing to follow through to the end and meet all deadlines."[12] A paralegal's reputation, adds Albrecht, rests on more than just results: "How you take a case from the initial client meeting to the settled and closed status shows every person in your office your abilities, skills, knowledge, determination, and commitment to be the client's service advocate."[13]

In addition, anyone who wants to be a paralegal must enjoy research. Paralegals often have to dig for that one piece of information that will win the case. They must also verify that information is correct before adding it to the client's file.

Relationships Are Key

Besides being effective researchers, paralegals must stay informed of changes in the laws that affect their company or clients, and be able to build relationships with others. Says Slaughter, "Paralegals must be team players."[14] Often, it is the paralegal's ability to gain

A paralegal takes notes with a voice recorder as she researches a case. Paralegals must have excellent research skills to help attorneys build a compelling case.

the cooperation of the various professionals who play a role in their client's case (for example, court clerks, witnesses, police officers, and private investigators) that helps the supervising attorney to win the case.

A paralegal who works in criminal law, for example, may need to interact with police officials to get copies of arrest reports, traffic collision reports, death reports, or stolen vehicle reports. Unfortunately, police and criminal lawyers have a long history of distrusting each other. Police officers often view criminal lawyers as more interested in freeing their clients than in seeing justice served, so the criminal law paralegal must be incredibly respectful, patient, and engaging to get the information he or she needs from the police in a timely manner.

Likewise, paralegals must be able to communicate clearly what they need. When hiring a private investigator to do research, for example, the paralegal must ensure the investigator is given the information that he or she needs to proceed. As investigator Joe Coyle notes, knowing exactly what the lawyer wants him to uncover helps him to do his job: "The paralegal should try to give me everything he or she knows about the case, including notes from the client's interview, any witness information, and what issues the attorney handling the case seeks to prove or disprove. If I know about certain important areas the attorney wants covered, I can focus my attention on them."[15]

Supervising lawyers also expect paralegals to have excellent communication skills, which they will use when interacting with clients. A lawyer may have the time to meet with a client only once or twice during a case, so he or she relies on paralegals to develop a positive working relationship with clients. Most attorneys handle the initial client interview and then hand the case to their paralegal, who then stays in touch with the client until the case is settled. Sometimes paralegals must hold a client's hand, says Estrin: "Warmth, compassion, and the highest quality of work product are imperative. Your clients are not generally calling you because everything in their lives is working properly. These are usually situations of a person in crisis."[16]

E-mail as "E-evidence"

One aspect of a paralegal's job is to collect evidence that will help his or her lawyer to prepare for court. As e-evidence, which includes computer-generated data such as e-mail, spreadsheets, and computer backup files, has become an effective tool for proving intent in law cases, it is a new area with which paralegals must become familiar. In her article "Ten Things Every Paralegal Must Know About Electronic Evidence," Regina Chepalis explains why e-evidence is an effective tool for proving a fact:

E-evidence, especially e-mail, has been called "the smoking gun of the future" based on its inherent potential to contain relevant information. E-mail users are often lulled into a false sense of security, believing that their messages can be easily deleted, or that they have some right of privacy in messages sent from their company computers to personal friends or family members. This sense of security causes the writers to let down their guard and converse more casually—often resulting in the revelation of damaging information. But these messages are neither transient nor private. They are as permanent and public as if the information were printed out on company letterhead.

Computer Skills a Must

Technological savvy is another skill set lawyers expect of paralegals. Paralegals typically use computer software throughout their workday to complete many of their tasks. For example, paralegals involved in litigation (lawsuits) use software to track the status of their client cases. Online case management systems enable the paralegals to manage correspondence, phone calls, billable hours, court dates, and action items that need to be addressed. As a lawyer might ask for a piece of information from a client file at any time, paralegals must be meticulous in keeping the files current.

Paralegals also spend many hours at their desks or in the library searching CD-ROM and Internet databases for information. As technology is continually changing, a willingness to keep learning is vital to a paralegal's success. As legal support manager Casey Anderson explains, "Each paralegal is faced with continually maintaining a high level of expertise on whatever is currently the 'state of the art.' They must routinely explore new hardware and software as it becomes available and try to integrate it into their daily work routine where appropriate."[17]

Marcy Jankovich, a claims specialist for a professional liability insurance company, adds that she would be hard-pressed to do her job without her PalmPilot. This mobile computing device allows her to store legal files, correspondence, and her appointment calendar, helping her to manage legal malpractice claims in three states as she travels. Says Jankovich, "I can't carry my paper files with me to court in Ohio to review documents for another case in Michigan. It just becomes too cumbersome."[18]

Varied Roles

Paralegals work in many areas of the law, such as personal injury, corporate, criminal, labor, intellectual property, entertainment, family, environmental, bankruptcy, patent, real estate, immigration, and employee benefits. As the law becomes increasingly complex, many paralegals choose to specialize in one area. Geography often plays a role in that choice, according to the AAfPE: "Each region experiences its own ebb and flow in the development of legal specializations. A high demand for expertise in immigration law may currently exist in California, for exam-

A paralegal uses a computer and law books to conduct research. Paralegals must be computer proficient to access information stored in electronic databases.

ple, but less so in Oklahoma, where the law surrounding oil and gas development or Native American issues may have greater urgency."[19]

A paralegal's specialization may narrow even further depending on his or her employer. For example, a paralegal working for a corporation may manage shareholder agreements and stock option plans, while a paralegal working for a government agency might prepare materials that explain policy, laws, or regulations. Paralegals employed by large companies that have their own legal departments may specialize in corporate regulation, customs, trademarks, copyrights, construction defects, merchandising, financial services, or franchising. If a paralegal works exclusively with labor law cases he or she may further specialize and handle only employee benefits issues. There is virtually no end to the degree of specialization.

Beating Burnout and Getting Ahead

Although those who persist in the profession and who are willing to work overtime are often rewarded with promotion, many paralegals still experience burnout. In addition, paralegals risk succumbing to boredom if their job consists of repetitive chores that fail to challenge them. Thus, it is critical to set career goals and evaluate them often, says Slaughter:

Discovery Procedures

One phase of litigation in which paralegals often participate is discovery, the process by which information related to a lawsuit is gathered. Paralegals and lawyers alike use four tools during discovery: depositions, requests for production, interrogatories, and requests for admission.

While conducting a deposition, paralegals and lawyers for both sides ask the parties involved questions that help to build their case. The answers to the questions are given under oath. If the person answering the questions (deponent) answers one way during a deposition and another way in court, the deposition can be shown to the jury to show that the witness changed his or her answers. In a request for production, one party in the lawsuit asks the other for physical evidence. This might include employment files, billing records, tax filings, wills, and other documents. Interrogatories are written questions that one party sends to the other. These must be answered under oath—and can also be used in court to challenge a witness. Requests for admission are when one party asks the opposing party to ascertain, under oath, that facts are true.

To have enjoyment in the profession, you need to want to be here. I recommend that new paralegals reevaluate their goals after two years. It's perfectly fine to remain a paralegal, but if you really want to be a lawyer, or you're not enjoying the job, you need to move on. Don't wait and realize five years down the road that you're stuck in a career you don't want to be in.[20]

Paralegals can acquire more challenging tasks by building relationships with in-house lawyers who can offer better assignments. Or they can request to move to another department. Paralegals often try out several jobs before finding the perfect fit. Paralegals in small firms sometimes find that the only way to get more interesting assignments is to move to a larger firm.

A smaller number of paralegals find that management offers the challenge they want. Paralegal managers typically supervise, recruit, train, and evaluate the performance of paralegal staff. As a manager for a law firm, Brad J. Baber explains, it is his job to match projects to each paralegal's expertise and experience:

> Presumably, past performance and matching the right personalities plays into the equation as well. This is often referred to as the "paralegal pool" concept in staffing. In other firms, paralegals are permanently assigned to teams or practice groups. The group then assumes the responsibility for keeping the work flowing to their assigned paralegals. In this instance, the paralegal manager might step in only when additional help is needed at peak times by temporarily assigning paralegals from slower areas to help out in the interim.[21]

Becoming a manager is often a matter of creating the position while continuing to fulfill previously assigned duties. Says Estrin, "There are no schools and few, if any, seminars to prepare you for the role; no real on-the-job tutelage specific to the position exists; and many firms still have to be convinced they need the position."[22]

Striking Out Alone

Some paralegals opt to open their own businesses, offering their services to anyone who needs them. It is an attractive option, yet in an article for *Legal Assistant Today*, Stacey Hunt and Veronica DeCoster note that paralegals should not jump into freelancing without first gaining law firm experience:

> No amount of education can substitute for hands-on training in managing case files, meeting local court requirements, and knowing, without being told, the necessary procedural steps to accomplish your task. Given the nature of freelance work, your attorney clients will not have time to hold your hand, and you will be expected to work with minimal supervision. Law firm experience also exposes you to many different personalities and styles. This will teach you to be more adaptable to the quirks of your attorney clients.[23]

To test the waters, paralegals often take on freelance projects while working full-time for a law firm or other employer. In doing so, they must ensure that the freelance projects do not conflict with cases of their full-time employer, which would be a breach of ethics. To eliminate this possibility, says Jankovich, "Usually, the firm would run a conflicts check, but before a freelancer could be hired to work on a project, he or she must be able to assure the potential employer that there will be no ethical conflict."[24]

One benefit of working independently is the opportunity to set their own hours and fees. Says Jankovich:

> How you structure your business is up to you. I had retainer contracts the firm had to sign that guaranteed my rates in writing. You want to know in advance that the attorney is going to pay your rate. If I worked in state court, for example, I charged $45 an hour. If I worked in federal court I charged $65 an hour. One contract guaranteed twenty

A paralegal and an attorney review information for a case. Some paralegals attend law school and become attorneys themselves.

hours of work a week and health insurance. It's all up to what you want to negotiate, but it's really up to the person needing your services.[25]

Though she enjoyed the freedom freelancing offered, Jankovich says she did not enjoy running her business:

Those hours spent upgrading your computer, creating statements of account, collections (attorneys sometimes do not want to pay you) and bookkeeping are not billable to anyone. There is also no one to prioritize when two different people need things at the same time. You sometimes simply have to work that 12-hour day to get it done. There is no one else to take over because you are sick, or stressed or have child care issues. I worked out of my home office. One day I realized that I never really "went home" from work.[26]

Outlook

Paralegal salaries are driven by education, training, and experience, as well as the size and geographic location of the employer. According to the Bureau of Labor Statistics, the 2002 median salary of a full-time paralegal was $37,950, while the top 10 percent earned more than $61,150. In 2002 the National Federation of Paralegal Associations conducted a survey of two thousand of its members. It found that 96 percent of paralegals are female. Seventy-one percent work for law firms, while 17 percent work for corporations. And 41 percent had bachelor's degrees, 33 percent had earned associate's degrees, and 58 percent had earned the CLA credential.

Most paralegals realize that their support of lawyers is very important. Says paralegal educator Stephen McEvoy: "The attorney-paralegal relationship is similar to the relationship between doctors and nurses."[27] Jankovich points out that the challenge of doing the job well keeps many paralegals committed to honing that relationship: "I love my job. I go home so brain dead, but I'm having so much fun. Every case has different issues. In a given day I might jump from tax problems to domestic relations problems to business contracts to criminal law. It's always a dance."[28]

Chapter 2

Lawyers

Lawyers play a unique role in society. In addition to prosecuting and defending people accused of crimes, some lawyers practice civil law and represent clients in transactions and contracts as well as with taxes, estate planning, and mortgages. Some offer clients advice on how to write a will, while others guide clients through the legal requirements of setting up a new company.

To be successful in practicing either criminal or civil law, lawyers must approach their tasks with a commitment to high ethical standards. Although motivated (and paid) to vigorously defend his or her clients' interests, a lawyer's job is first to uphold the law. Other attributes needed by successful lawyers include sound reasoning and problem-solving skills, a good memory, and well-honed listening and communication skills.

Beyond the type of law they choose to practice, job satisfaction depends, in large part, on a lawyer's working environment. While the American Bar Foundation Lawyer Statistical Report notes that more than 60 percent of the nearly 1 million lawyers in the United States work in large law firms that accept a variety of cases, some lawyers prefer to work in small "boutique" firms that focus on a single area of law, such as patent law or workers' compensation. Some lawyers relish the challenge of building their own practices, while others enjoy working as part of a large corporation's in-house legal department. The types of cases a lawyer handles is another factor in job satisfaction. Based on their interests, some choose to work on behalf of the government, while others seek employment in religious organizations, real estate agencies, banks or public utilities.

Wherever he or she works, a lawyer's behavior is tightly regulated by court rules, laws, and professional ethics. The ABA declares that admirable lawyers dedicate themselves to serving others honestly, competently, and responsibly—and commit to improving the fairness and quality of justice in the legal system.

Law School: The Most Common Route

In order to become lawyers, most people must attend law school and earn a Juris Doctor (JD). Traditionally, this takes three years of full-time study. Some students who wish to continue working while they study attend school at night, but it can take up to five years to graduate from part-time studies. The ABA is responsible for accrediting law schools and has approved the curriculum of more than 180 law schools across the country.

The ABA's accreditation standards are rigorous, and the expected curriculum is clearly spelled out. In law school students learn the basics of legal writing and research, contracts, property, and criminal and constitutional law. The curriculum also gives students a sound understanding of American and world history, political thought and theory, economics, and basic finance. Some

An attorney confers with a client in her office. Displayed on the back wall of the office is the attorney's Juris Doctor diploma.

A law school graduate receives a sash during commencement proceedings. Law school graduates must pass a state bar exam before they can practice law.

law students enroll in joint degree programs. Upon graduation, they receive a second advanced degree, such as a Master of Business Administration, in addition to their law degree. This is particularly helpful if they intend to practice as an in-house lawyer for a large corporation.

The ABA dictates that to enter law school, students need an undergraduate college degree. The ABA, however, does not recommend that students choose specific undergraduate degrees. Its reasoning is that "the law is too multifaceted, and the human mind too adaptable, to permit such a linear approach to preparing for law school or the practice of law."[29] But the ABA does require that all applicants to accredited law schools take a rigorous standardized test known as the Law School Admission Test (LSAT). The LSAT, which evaluates an applicant's reasoning skills, is a sufficient tool to weed out those who would not succeed in law school. The LSAT is scored on a scale from 120 to 180, with 151 being the average score. In addition, test takers are assigned a percentile ranking based on the percentage of students with scores below theirs. Typically, law schools take students with the highest scores. A student who scores poorly can retake the test, according to StudentMarket.com, but since many law schools average the test scores together, "Most people are better off preparing thoroughly for the test, taking it one time and getting their top score."[30]

The LSAT helps to measure aptitude; law school itself provides training. However, before they can practice law, all would-be lawyers must pass a state bar examination, which gives them license to practice in that state. The Multistate Bar Exam, a very challenging test, includes two hundred multiple choice questions in six subject areas: contracts, torts, constitutional law, real property, evidence, and criminal law/procedure. The number of questions that must be answered correctly varies by region and year, with complex formulas used to determined a passing score.

Further, would-be lawyers must pass a character review called a moral fitness test. A state's Board of Bar Examiners extensively researches the would-be lawyer's background to determine whether he or she should be allowed to practice. *Detroit News* reporter Marisa Schultz explains how invasive the review is:

> Applicants must self-report, in a half-inch thick application packet, their criminal, driving, financial, legal, health and educational history. They also must be fingerprinted and pay for an official criminal and driving record background check. . . . Common grounds for denial include criminal conduct, drug or alcohol abuse, mental or emotional instability, a history of bad debts or financial irresponsibility, employment terminations and involvement in civil litigation.[31]

If the applicant passes the review, a final formality is the taking of an oath to uphold the law.

An Enlightening Detour

Many law students decide to enter law school directly after their undergraduate study. Yet attorney Joel Wattenbarger notes that some people take time to gain real-world law experience: "It's not an uncommon experience for people who think they might like a career in law to work as a paralegal before they go to law school."[32] Not only do paralegal positions give would-be lawyers experience in the law, they help recent graduates discover whether or not they really want to be lawyers. Those who decide being a lawyer is not for them have wisely saved themselves from investing years of effort and many thousands of dollars in law school tuition.

Many law firms allocate a number of paralegal slots for this purpose. The slots are called transitional paralegal positions (as compared to career paralegal positions). Transitional paralegals are expected to work hard and bring excellent organizational and writing skills to their tasks. They also need to display a willing-

Tips for Passing the LSAT

The Law School Admission Test (LSAT) measures a person's ability to reason. This is not necessarily something for which most college graduates are prepared, according to StudentMarket.com, a Web site that offers LSAT preparation software. The key to doing well on the test is to read the questions carefully, looking for patterns and relationships:

Although time is strictly limited on the LSAT, working too quickly can also damage your score. Many problems hinge on subtle points, and most require careful reading of the setup. Because undergraduate school puts such heavy reading loads on students, many will follow their academic conditioning and read the questions quickly, looking only for the gist of what the question is asking. Once they have found it, they mark their answer and move on, confident they have answered it correctly. Later, many are startled to discover that they missed questions because they either misread the problems or overlooked subtle points.

To do well in your undergraduate classes, you had to attempt to solve every, or nearly every, problem on a test. Not so with the LSAT. In fact, if you try to solve every problem on this test you will probably decimate your score. For the vast majority of people, the key to performing well on the LSAT is not the number of questions they answer, within reason, but the percentage they answer correctly.

A paralegal and an attorney research information in law books. Working as a paralegal helps some would-be lawyers decide if a career in law is right for them.

ness to do whatever is asked of them. As paralegal manager Nancy Slaughter explains, "It's my job to hire these people and to give them good assignments, but it's their job to give me a can-do attitude. They should be willing to do anything that I ask."[33]

Numerous Niches

The transitional paralegal position is purposely structured to give the employee a broad exposure to the law. Without this real-world experience, graduates often have a harder time deciding on a specialty. The real danger, says lawyer Gary Munneke, is not that new lawyers will fail to find jobs, but that they will find the wrong ones: "A high percentage of law graduates change jobs within the first two years of graduation. . . . Part of the problem is that until you actually try something, it is difficult to know if you will like it."[34]

Legal consultant Phil J. Shuey suggests that would-be lawyers carefully assess their strengths as they prepare for their career:

> Some lawyers are naturally at ease with clients; others are more comfortable away from human interaction, instead creating or generating the work product for the client. Some lawyers enjoy negotiation, mediation, and resolution of conflicts. Other lawyers embrace adversarial work—they enjoy the "battle" of the courtroom. The problem solving involved in complex litigation or transactional issues may be attractive to other practitioners. Carefully evaluate those tasks at which you are good.[35]

Specialization Benefits Clients

Although many lawyers are generalists, handling whatever cases come their way, others specialize, believing that by doing so they are better able to provide clients with competent legal care. Probate lawyers, for instance, are experts in writing wills and settling estates. Maritime lawyers handle legal issues relating to navigation and shipping, including property damage and personal injuries. Intellectual property lawyers ensure that clients are protected from those who would steal their ideas. Securities lawyers guard the investments of average citizens and see to it that corporations abide by federal and state regulations over trading in stocks and bonds. Real estate lawyers help to make certain that property is passed from one owner to another legally. The list of specialties and subspecialties is virtually endless.

Specialists may work within a law firm or be employed directly by a corporation to handle legal issues affecting its business. Depending on the size of the corporation, in-house legal departments may consist of a single attorney or be staffed with hundreds of lawyers. While in-house lawyers usually do not carry caseloads as large as those carried by lawyers working in private firms, they interact with a wide array of internal clients. In a typical week, for example, they may meet with the company's sales reps, president, and unionized factory workers on various issues.

Advances Aid the Disabled

Thanks to advances in technology, persons with disabilities who wish to be lawyers are able to handle tasks that they previously could not. Lawyers with vision problems, for instance, can request that documents be scanned into Braille. Lawyers who are hearing impaired can follow court proceedings via real-time transcription services provided by court reporters during trials, and lawyers whose physical disabilities make them unable to type can use voice-recognition software that transforms their spoken words into type on their computer.

Private Versus Public

More numerous than the attorneys working in the corporate world are those who specialize in criminal law. This is because the justice system at the local, state, and federal levels employs lawyers called prosecutors, or district attorneys, to argue criminal cases in court. When someone is accused of a crime, it is the job of the prosecutor to use evidence provided by the police to prove the defendant's guilt. Yet prosecutors must also be alert to signs that someone accused of a crime is not guilty, such as conflicting testimony or improper police work.

Public defenders (PDs), on the other hand, are criminal lawyers who represent accused individuals who cannot afford legal representation. The government foots the bill, as common law guarantees every citizen the right to a fair and speedy trial. Attorney Barbara Arrants describes her experience as a PD:

> A public defender's life is thrilling, exciting, stressful, thankless, impossible, and wonderful—all rolled into one. As a general sessions attorney I would walk into court every morning, court docket in hand, with some 15 to 25 names highlighted. These were my clients for the day, many of whom I would meet for the first time in court. Needless to say, you have to be able to think on your feet. I would meet and talk with each of my clients for a few minutes, then go

into the courtroom for the call of the docket. After docket call, I met with the district attorneys. As a result of this meeting, I marked some cases for trial, some for a bond-reduction hearing, some for plea-bargain offers, and some for bind-over hearings. I stayed in court all day until all of the cases were disposed of. I handled all of the hearings, trials, and pleas that day. This goes on every day, five days a week.[36]

Arrants adds that while public defenders do not enjoy the prestige and high salaries of lawyers working in private firms, she minded this less than the perception that firm lawyers offer better skills:

In 2002 a public defender advises a ten-year-old boy on his rights during a preliminary hearing on his alleged involvement in a crime.

What I disliked was fighting the stereotype that PDs are lousy lawyers simply because they work for indigent clients. In fact, in most cases the opposite is true. Most of the PDs I know are exceptional attorneys. Like me, they graduated in the top part of their class and do this type of work because they enjoy it, not because they couldn't get any other job. The main difference between a PD and a hired attorney is the amount of money available for expert witnesses, tests, exhibits, and the like. . . . The quality of the attorney is essentially the same, however.[37]

Personality Matters

Although their legal knowledge is critical, above all else lawyers must pay attention to how they come across to others. Lawyers lacking people skills do not go far. In particular, they must interact well with support staff, gaining the cooperation of paralegals, secretaries, and librarians. Similarly, lawyers need to display positive interpersonal skills in order to win the trust of their clients and the respect of judges and juries. In *Full Disclosure*, attorney Christen Civiletto Carey shares why actions matter, both in and out of court:

Do not let your frustration with the process or the judge's ruling spill over into your dealings with the judge's secretary, clerks, or other personnel. These people have day-to-day contact with the judge and will often tell the judge about a particularly good or bad experience with a lawyer. Act in a professional manner from the moment you arrive at the courthouse. Often you will come into contact with jurors, and your behavior will begin to shape their perception of you or the judicial experience in which they are about to participate.[38]

Interviewing Well

People skills are also noted and critiqued during job interviews. Carey notes that behaviors that fall into the category of good manners are what those who are hiring tend to look for. Not even excellent credentials will save a candidate who seems rude or lacking in social skills. Especially bad is being tardy for the interview.

An attorney questions a witness as he presents a bag of cocaine as evidence. Lawyers must demonstrate strong interpersonal skills, particularly when questioning witnesses.

Writer Donna Gerson shares this scenario:

> Dan, a 2L [second-year law student] and law review staff member, received a call-back interview with a large firm. He arrived 20 minutes late for his interview, apologizing profusely for traffic jams and parking woes. Bottom line: no offer. Jane, a 3L [third-year law student] awaiting her initial interview with the hiring partner of a mid-sized firm, treated the receptionist brusquely. When the receptionist tried to engage Jane in conversation, she muttered one-word responses and avoided eye contact. Result: no offer. Despite good credentials, neither Dan nor Jane received job offers, because they failed to mind their manners. In a nutshell, minding your manners means thinking of others and being

a considerate human being. Lawyers seek good manners in their employees. Why? In a service-based profession that thrives on personal relationships and involves interaction with individuals of varying degrees of wealth, social standing, and knowledge, a lawyer must be able to behave politely under a variety of circumstances.[39]

The First Few Years

Although many lawyers working in law firms dream of becoming a rainmaker—a lawyer who brings in substantial business—new lawyers should concentrate on learning the ropes. For first-year lawyers in private firms, that means accepting lots of grunt

Ambulance Chasers

The derogatory term ambulance chasers *usually refers to attorneys who specialize in representing people injured in accidents. While they do not actually chase ambulances, successful personal-injury attorneys often must go to some effort to find clients. In his book* Order in the Court, *lawyer David Mullally explains how some of these specialty lawyers use less-than-savory tactics to solicit clients:*

Some have a system in place that funnels the clients to them. Some employ private investigators that show up at the hospital, allegedly "investigating" the accident, wanting only to interview the victim. During the course of the interview, the investigator will try to route the victim to the attorney the investigator is working for. Other attorneys have relationships with paramedics who are already in the ambulance, or with staff in hospitals, tow-truck drivers and auto-repair garages, doctors, chiropractors and others who just "happen" to have the attorney's card to give to the accident victim. One enterprising attorney I know opened his office next door to a funeral home. He would dress nicely and regularly attend funeral services of people who died in accidents. He would meet the family members, offer his condolences and suggest they visit his office after the service to discuss the compensation they may be entitled to from the death of their loved one. He was very successful.

work—tasks that a secretary or paralegal could easily coordinate, such as handling depositions, contacting court reporters, preparing witness profiles and folders, and filing papers with the court clerk.

New lawyers must demonstrate enthusiasm for an assignment if they want to get off on the right foot with senior members of the firm (sometimes called partners), even if the task means putting in overtime. Carey describes a typical scenario: "Late in the week, your partner calls you on the telephone. She relates that she promised the client a written work product by Monday afternoon and wants to know if you can handle it. Make no mistake, that is a statement, not a question. First, respond with: 'I'll be right there.'"[40] To successfully handle these requests, new lawyers must ask for deadlines, suggestions for where to start research, and exactly what product the partner or senior lawyer expects them to deliver, such as a memorandum, oral report, or outline.

In comparison to what new lawyers experience, second-through fourth-year lawyers begin to grasp the nuances of practicing law. They start by reading the Federal Rules of Civil Procedure, the state civil practice rules, and any local court rules, so that they understand the basics of filing, prosecuting, and defending an action. They also become generally familiar with their in-house library's resources and build professional relationships with the law library staff.

Job Stresses

Many lawyers say that the main attraction of their job is the chance to help others. The downside, however, is the need to put in long hours to properly manage their caseloads. New lawyers, in particular, find they have little time for a social life, or even sleep. Many lawyers feel isolated and overwhelmed. At least one study has shown that one-third of lawyers suffer from depression, alcohol or drug abuse, obsessive behavior, or social alienation. Many complain that their personal relationships are skewed or inadequate. Some are so busy working that they do not have the time to build and nurture personal relationships.

Showtime

Regardless of the issues in their private lives, when lawyers enter the courtroom they must be able to give their total focus to rep-

A lawyer relaxes from research with a nap. Long working hours are common for attorneys new to the profession.

resenting their client. This is just one skill they hone with practice. While new lawyers in smaller firms typically get the opportunity to handle a court case sooner than those working in large firms, eventually they all argue their first case. New lawyers have much to learn beyond the intricacies of arguing a case. Although experienced lawyers know to be respectful in court, many employ tricks that are designed to sway the judge and jurors to their client's favor. A lawyer might dress in rumpled clothing or carry a tattered briefcase to draw sympathy. Lawyers make sure that nothing in their behavior can be interpreted as disrespectful or in any way distracting to the jury. For example, some lawyers remove their watch to ensure they do not unconsciously glance at it and convey to the jury that they hope to rush the proceedings.

The courtroom experience is bound by numerous rules of conduct. Opposing lawyers, for example, may not address each other unless directly given permission to do so by the judge. Likewise, lawyers may not approach the judge or a witness without permission. Carey advises lawyers against sighing, complaining, or making faces if a judge rules against their client, since this could motivate the judge to find them in contempt of court: "Instead, thank

A jury listens as an attorney presents evidence. A trial attorney's demeanor in the courtroom can influence the jury's verdict.

the judge or say 'yes, your honor' and, if no exception for the record is needed, move on. Don't argue with the judge, but do take up certain matters in the appropriate context or through the correct procedural channels."[41]

Outlook

Although some people say there are too many lawyers, it remains a popular career choice. In fact, in 2003 more than 145,088 students were enrolled in ABA-approved law schools, an increase of 3 percent from 2002. The compensation for all the years of schooling and abiding by rules that at times can seem confining is that lawyers on average earn a very comfortable income. Some lawyers will make more than others, but the median annual earnings of lawyers in 2002, according to the Bureau of Labor Statistics, was $90,290.

Perhaps Reinhardt sums up the impact lawyers have on society when he says that

> it's not just the billable hours that matter, it's not just their ability to attract business—that the height of the profession is not being a rainmaker. We can tell them that it's the quality of their performance as a professional, as a member of a group charged with a unique trust and responsibility that counts at least as heavily—that it [is] the amount that they give back to their communities, their nation, and their profession.[42]

Making career choices is never easy, says Munneke, but "on the positive side, in this complex, interconnected, global, and changing society, people are confronted with legal problems in everything they do. As long as there are legal problems, society will need people with legal training."[43]

Chapter 3

Judges

Under the U.S. Constitution, anyone who goes to court is guaranteed a fair trial, and it is the judge's job to see that this guarantee is fulfilled. Judges oversee many types of cases—from traffic offenses to matters of life and death. In hearing each case, a judge must ensure that the court delivers justice while also safeguarding the legal rights of those charged who enter the courtroom.

Most judges began their careers as lawyers. For many lawyers, serving as a judge is the highlight of their careers. Says Judge James Lanuti: "Being a judge has its advantages and disadvantages over being a lawyer. The advantage is that it is a somewhat prestigious position and you have the respect in the community. Lawyers are often the victims of jokes but judges are highly respected. It's amazing to me how a lawyer becomes extremely wise once he or she becomes a judge."[44]

Each judge, however, eventually proves through his or her actions whether this respect is justified. The attributes that predict success as a judge are the same, regardless of the level at which a judge serves, be it local, state, or federal. To succeed, judges must bring a number of traits to the job. These include the ability to sort through information and to look at issues objectively. Another is the ability to listen well. Says Judge Lisa White Hardwick, "My basic approach to being a judge is to listen to the facts, listen carefully to the facts, listen to both sides; don't prejudge anyone or any issue . . . and to apply the law to those facts and to do what the law requires."[45]

Judges are either elected or appointed, depending on the court. Many judges serve fixed, renewable terms. Often, a judge is appointed to fill an immediate vacancy. After serving this initial term, he or she may seek to be elected to the position or decide to run for a position in a higher court. Most state and federal judges make their rulings in court, but those presiding over appellate (appeals) courts do not hold trials. Instead, appellate judges base their decisions on the transcripts from the lower trial court and sometimes a short oral argument from each side's attorney. Appellate judge Richard Brown says the job requires a lot of writing in isolation: "There's not a lot of interaction with the public and if you don't like to write law, forget it. In fact, if you don't love the law, forget it."[46]

Qualifications

In addition to having this passion for the law, judges must have at a minimum a bachelor's degree and applicable work experience. And although approximately forty states allow persons who have not passed the bar to hold limited-jurisdiction judgeships, most state and federal judges are required to be lawyers. David Mullally explains:

A judge listens as opposing attorneys argue a point of law. One of a judge's chief responsibilities is to rule on such points during trial.

Almost all judges, both state and federal, were practicing attorneys prior to appointment or election. A large percentage were prosecuting attorneys, which reflects a strong public preference for those that enforce laws and lock up criminals to preside as judges. Appellate judges often served as trial judges prior to appointment to the appellate bench.[47]

Like lawyers, judges are held to ethical rules and a code of judicial conduct. Yet some judges behave as if they were above the law. Some become too lazy or perhaps too sure of their popularity to care about putting in the research and contemplation needed to make sound rulings. Others allow their personal biases against certain people and situations to cloud their judgment,

In 2004 a judge listens to testimony from a defendant on trial for leaving the scene of an auto accident involving a pedestrian.

while still others are more interested in catering to special interest groups that have the political power to get them reelected than they are in ensuring that justice is served. These judges do not deserve to keep their power.

Most judges, however, are dedicated and conduct themselves professionally. They understand that their rulings affect the lives of many people—not just those who stand before them in court. Children, for example, are affected by a judge's decision to remove them from a harmful environment. Because of this power, Judge Judy Sheindlin says that she takes her role very seriously:

> In family court, judges make life and death decisions every day. We face challenges every bit as daunting as those facing a team of surgeons: Do we return children to their parents? Will they be safe? Was the baby's arm broken during a fall, or did Mom break it in frustration? Do we deny Dad's visitation with his kids because Mom claims he abused them? Do we give a fifteen-year-old probation, or are the risks to the community too high? If judges make mistakes in these and countless other cases, the results can be life threatening.[48]

Training

To help judges become comfortable with making these types of decisions, all states have some type of orientation for newly elected or appointed judges, and many states require judges to enroll in continuing education courses while they serve on the bench. General and continuing education courses typically last from a couple of days to several weeks. Judges can also take advantage of online tutorials that more easily fit into their schedules. The Judicial Education Center, for example, offers municipal judges training in a variety of subjects, including search warrants, intoxicated drivers, domestic violence, and ethics. Training is important not only because judges hear heavy caseloads, but because advances in technology have made cases increasingly complex.

Order in the Court

Another task that judges quickly learn through training and experience is to effectively manage their courts. While they must

Contempt of Court

While court is in session, if a judge feels a lawyer, jury member, or court visitor is improperly challenging or ignoring the court's authority, the judge may declare the defiant person (contemnor) to be in contempt of court. Contempt of court is defined as any willful disobedience, disregard of a court order, or misconduct in court, such as yelling at a judge or refusing to be quiet. The judge has the authority to fine contemnors or have them removed from court and placed in jail.

follow a standard protocol regarding the structure of the trial, individual judges are very much in charge of the general atmosphere of their courts. As each judge sets up rules of conduct that he or she feels maintains respect in their courtroom, that atmosphere can vary widely. Some courtrooms feel very relaxed; others, extremely formal. As well, some judges are very territorial about their courtrooms. Some, for instance, do not allow television cameras to be present. Others require that those who come to observe a trial pass through metal detectors or be photographed.

As most judges were previously lawyers, some choose to establish rules specific to the behavior of lawyers. Some, for instance, do not allow lawyers to place their briefcases on the table. Instead, the briefcases must be placed on the floor. Other judges request that lawyers remain outside the well (the area of the courtroom between the judge's bench and counsel's table) unless they are given permission to enter. Television programs often depict this, with lawyers asking, "Permission to approach the bench, Your Honor?"

Judges also demand respect from defendants. If a defendant decides to be disruptive—shouting, stomping his or her feet, moaning, pounding on the table, or refusing to remain seated— the judge can order the defendant to be shackled or gagged. The judge may even decide to remove the defendant if he or she continues to disrupt court proceedings. Some courts offer adjoining soundproof rooms with closed-circuit television so that defendants can be removed yet still be granted their constitutional right to confront their accusers.

Varied Tasks

Although they spend many hours presiding over trials, judges spend much of their time in other activities. For example, during pretrial hearings (arraignments), they listen to allegations (charges against someone) and determine whether there is enough evidence of guilt to justify a trial. In criminal cases, judges sometimes decide that persons charged with crimes should be held in jail until their trial date.

Judges also spend time in their private offices (chambers) preparing for trials. In doing so, they read documents on pleadings and motions, research legal issues, and write opinions. They usually are assisted by one or more law clerks who help them conduct research for court cases.

Case Assignments

When in court, judges typically preside over the same courtroom every day. Each day, the judge is notified of the cases that he or

A judge presiding over a trial listens to two attorneys who have approached the bench to discuss a legal point.

she has been assigned. Likewise, a daily calendar is posted on each judge's courtroom door so that people know where to go for their hearings. The calendar is a helpful tool in that it contains the date, the judge's name, the type of proceeding (such as criminal, probate, family law), the case number (docket number), the names of the parties involved, and the attorneys' names. If a defendant is being represented by a public defender (government lawyers assigned to those who cannot afford legal representation), the initials "PD" are noted instead of an attorney's name.

Judges are assigned cases by the presiding judge. Some defense lawyers, hoping to get their clients the lightest sentence possible, attempt to disqualify a judge from hearing their client's case if the judge has a reputation for being harsh. Sometimes the attorney is able to remove the judge for no reason, but usually he or she must provide sufficient reason to disqualify a judge. If this happens, the case is assigned to another judge. Judges can also remove (recuse) themselves from a case. They might do this if they are friends with one of the parties, or if some other circumstance exists that might prevent them from being objective during the trial.

Once the case is assigned, the judge and attorneys discuss any trial motions, such as if one side wants to exclude evidence before the opposing lawyer presents it to a jury. They also discuss how many days the trial will take, review the witness list, and assign the order in which the witnesses will be called.

Judges have some discretion regarding their schedule. Lanuti shares the duties he has during a typical week:

We have juries come in on Mondays and we schedule all our jury trials on that day. If we need more time, we can do it on Tuesday and Wednesday. I'm here by eight or eight-thirty to get ready for the day. My first court call is at nine. If the cases resolve themselves, I can sometimes finish in court at three, but if not I'll be there until five. When I finish early, I can use the time in chambers to familiarize myself with the next day's cal [caseload]. When I was a lawyer, I always appreciated a judge who took the time to be prepared, to read the papers that the lawyers had filed. That isn't always the case, but that's one thing as a judge I've always shot for and to do it requires a certain amount of homework.[49]

Passing the Bar

While *passing the bar* can mean that someone has passed a state bar exam and is now legally allowed to practice law, it has a different meaning in court. In the courtroom, the railing that separates the lawyer's tables from the spectator area is known as "the bar." Thus, the expression *passing the bar* can be taken literally: a lawyer can legally pass through the railing's swinging gate from the spectator's side and practice law. Someone who is not a lawyer does not have this right, unless he or she is a witness or party to a case and is directed to do so. A person who violates this rule would be instructed by the judge to leave immediately, or be removed by the bailiff, who is in charge of security in the courtroom.

Justice with Juries

As the U.S. Constitution guarantees a jury trial to any person accused of a crime that carries a maximum punishment of six months or longer in jail, in most criminal trials a jury decides the defendant's guilt or innocence. But the choice between a jury or bench trial (one decided by a judge) remains with the defendant.

If a defendant wants a jury, the judge assigned to the case supervises the selection of the jury in a process called voir dire. In this selection process, lawyers for both sides ask the potential jurors questions. Their intent is to try to identify and eliminate those who would likely decide against their client. The judge, too, might ask questions to clarify if there are reasons why a potential juror is unable to offer an unbiased ear.

Once the jury has been selected, judges in state courts explain to the jury that it must reach a verdict by a certain majority or unanimity of its members. In federal court, however, the judge directs the jury to reach a unanimous decision. Only when the jury members are in agreement are they to notify the judge that they have reached a verdict.

Judges do not hold private conversations with juries, but while in court, the judge speaks directly to the jury on how to

Jurors raise their hands as they vote on a verdict. Judges provide jurors with detailed instructions as to how to conduct verdict deliberations.

conduct its deliberations. These instructions help the jury to focus on the charges on which they are to decide. Mullally explains:

> The judge instructs the jury on the law applied in the case being tried. It's up to the attorneys to submit to the judge the law they believe applies. The attorneys and judge usually meet, sometimes in chambers with the court reporter, sometimes in open court with the jury present, to discuss each attorney's selection of what law they think applies. The attorneys may file briefs citing cases and the reasons they believe a particular jury instruction should be given. If there is a disagreement over certain instructions, then the judge makes a decision and each side can state their position on the record to preserve their objections for appeal.[50]

A Judge's Right

If the jury is not able to determine the defendant's guilt or innocence that day, the judge gives them more time. Some cases are

The Highest Court

Although each state has its own supreme court, the highest court in the United States is the Supreme Court. Nine justices sit on the court, appointed by the president of the United States with the consent of the Senate. In addition to reviewing decisions made in courts at the state level, the justices also consider issues related to the U.S. Constitution. Thousands of people send appeals to the Supreme Court for review each year, yet the justices accept fewer than two hundred due to time constraints. Typically, the justices accept cases that have the widest impact on the most citizens. These cases might involve right-to-life issues or threats to national security. Since the judges are appointed for life and may keep their positions as long as they exhibit good behavior, the Senate is very careful to review the past judgments of candidates. Some candidates decide this scrutiny infringes on their personal privacy and decline to continue the appointment process. However, it is quite an honor to sit on the Supreme Court, and of interest to judges who want the chance to make important legal decisions without the political headaches of reelection campaigns.

The highest court in the United States is the Supreme Court, composed of nine justices (pictured in 2003) appointed to life terms by the president.

so thoroughly covered in the media that a judge may decide that the jury cannot go home until it has made its decision. Thus, the judge sequesters the jury members so that they do not have the opportunity to speak with or be swayed by information they might receive from the media. If the case is complex, the judge can sequester the jury for the duration of the trial.

While the jury decides the facts of case, it is the judge who sets the sentencing. If a defendant is found guilty, the judge determines an appropriate punishment after reviewing several factors. The judge may, for instance, look at the defendant's past criminal record, his or her age, the circumstances of the crime, and whether the defendant appears to feel genuine remorse. Some judges prefer to follow mandatory sentencing laws, while others make their judgments on a case-by-case basis, fitting the punishment to the offender.

In cases where no jury is involved, the judge determines both fact and how the law will be applied to each case. Some judges become known for their leniency, while others, like Sheindlin, gain reputations for being tough. Sheindlin explains her stance in the courtroom:

> If I have learned one thing from our criminal justice system, it is that expediency breeds contempt. Especially among kids who think they can get away with murder every time they appear in court. I cannot speak for many of my colleagues, but I do not make deals with fourteen-year-olds. Lawyers are always asking me if I will cut some slack for their clients. If they plead guilty, will I parole them? Will I place them on probation? Will I accept a plea to a misdemeanor in exchange for their cooperation with a special youth program? My standard answer to all such offers: "This is not *Let's Make a Deal*, and I'm not Monty Hall!"[51]

Politics Play a Role

Throughout the trial process, the judge is supposed to remain impartial—that is, to not be influenced by outsiders, by his or her political opinions, or (in the case of judges who are elected) by the opinions of those who make campaign contributions. Unfortunately, as reelection costs rise, only those able to raise sufficient campaign

The U.S. Court System

COURTS OF LAST RESORT ON APPEAL

U.S. Supreme Court
Is free to accept or reject the cases it will hear, except in rare mandatory cases.

State Supreme Courts of Appeal
The final court of appeal for most state cases. If a case involves a right protected by U.S. Constitution, a party may appeal to the U.S. Circuit Court of Appeals.

INTERMEDIATE COURTS OF APPEAL

State Intermediate Courts of Appeal
The first court of appeals for most state cases. In 10 states the state Supreme Court is the only court of appeals.

U.S. Circuit Courts of Appeal (12 courts)
Reviews cases from the U.S. District Courts in its circuit. Appeals go to the U.S. Supreme Court.

U.S. Court of Appeals for the Federal Circuit (CAFC)
Reviews civil appeals dealing with minor claims against the U.S. govt., patent rights, and international trade disputes.

TRIAL COURTS

State Trial Courts
Almost all cases involving state civil and criminal laws are initially filed in state or local trial courts. Appeals usually go to the state intermediate court of appeals.

U.S. District Courts (94 courts)
Handle criminal and civil cases involving federal statutes or the U.S. Constitution, and civil cases between citizens from different states involving more than $75,000. Most appeals go to the U.S. Circuit Court of Appeals.

U.S. Court of International Trade
Specializes in cases that involve international trade. Appeals go to the CAFC.

U.S. Claims Court
For federal cases involving amounts over $10,000, conflicts from Indian Claims Commission, and cases involving some government contractors. Appeals go to the CAFC.

funds can compete. Reinhardt feels this reality has the potential to skew justice: "That judges must raise huge amounts of money if challenged, or that lawyers seeking to run for an open judicial post must spend in excess of $120,000 in order to run is outrageous. And who is interested in contributing to judicial elections, anyway—you guessed it, lawyers."[52]

Sheindlin notes that "all too often, justice is denied, largely because of the way we choose our judges in the first place. Too often, these appointments are based not on ability and wisdom, but on political expediency, payback, race, gender and other 'politically correct' criteria. That is absurd."[53]

Outlook

The salary range for judges varies widely depending upon their court and responsibilities. Federal court of appeals judges earned on average $164,100 a year in 2001, while district court judges averaged $154,700. Federal judges with limited jurisdiction, such as magistrates and bankruptcy court judges, averaged $142,324. A survey by the National Center for State Courts shows that annual salaries of associate justices of the highest state courts averaged $120,100 in 2002. Salaries of state intermediate appellate court judges averaged $116,064, while salaries of state judges of general jurisdiction trial courts averaged $109,811.

While judges typically earn less than lawyers, other benefits are tremendous. "People come to the court system because they can't resolve a problem on their own," notes Hardwick. "And we can provide them a best source of assistance."[54]

Chapter 4

Court Reporters

Court reporters, hired to accurately transcribe legal proceedings, are an essential part of the legal system. In a judicial setting, for example, appeals often rely on the court reporter's transcript. Approximately sixty thousand court reporters work in the United States. Some reporters are hired by the courts and work as full-time "official" reporters. When in court, these reporters usually sit just below the judge's bench, facing the witness stand. But many court reporters work outside the courtroom, freelancing for law offices, corporations, colleges, and media organizations. In doing so, they record speeches, conversations, legal proceedings, and meetings that require a formal written record. As court reporter

A court reporter, seated below the judge's bench, transcribes a trial's proceedings. The reporter's transcription constitutes the official record of all court cases.

Laura Hebb says, "Court reporters are a fly on the wall of history but people forget we are there. We are on the front lines."[55]

To be successful in their role of recording this history, court reporters need significant technical skill. While some reporters, like Connie Church, find a natural flow in building these skills, others find that learning to type as people speak (and often quite rapidly) takes many months of practice. Church shares how she was able to grasp court reporting so quickly: "The little machine intrigued me. I was a good typist and had studied shorthand so I understood the concept of writing by sound and syllable. . . . I enjoyed court reporting school and finished fairly quickly, thanks, I believe, in part to good finger dexterity from 11 years of piano lessons."[56]

Yet court reporters need other attributes as well. To capture an accurate record, court reporters utilize excellent listening skills, strong grammatical skills, concentration, and stamina. They must be able to take charge of the proceedings—to slow people down if they are talking too fast or prompt them to talk louder if they cannot be clearly heard. Court reporter Ellen Leach says, "I've learned to really be a diplomat. [I] must control the proceedings."[57] Yet when in court they must be deferential toward the judge, who is in charge of the courtroom.

Similarly, they must be able to remain professional, even when cases are unpleasant to hear. In a murder or child molestation case, for example, the court reporter must be able to detach his or her emotions from the proceedings.

Court reporters also need to be flexible. Church explains:

> Mostly you'll be in comfortable conference rooms. But you'll also report depositions in cramped doctors' offices, practically knee to knee with the attorneys and witnesses; or offices at any kind of business you can think of, including heavy equipment operators, gravel pits, shipyards, etc. I've also reported depositions at churches, prisons, schools, pool halls and hotels, and several times in a dying person's bedroom. Once I even set up my machine in a parking lot and reported a conference with a judge over an attorney's car speakerphone. You must be able to adapt to all of these reporting situations. Your attitude in handling jobs like

Telephone Depositions

Court reporters can conduct depositions (interview with a witness) over the telephone, according to the National Court Reporters Association, except in states that have rules dictating that the reporter must conduct the deposition in the presence of the witness.

Although most states permit telephone depositions, court reporters typically conduct them only when necessary. That is because they can be a frustrating experience: Court reporters must deal with garbled speech, poor phone connections, and the difficulty of trying to decipher which participant is speaking if more than one person is on the call.

these makes a difference in whether or not you are hired by these attorneys in the future.[58]

Becoming a Court Reporter

Court reporting requires formal training, but not a college degree. For those who want both, however, many two- and four-year colleges offer programs accredited by the National Court Reporters Association (NCRA). One court reporter notes how an academic background helps her to be a better court reporter:

[Every course] you take will work in court reporting. A typical week for me, if we are on general trial, could include a little bit of everything. We could have a criminal case where a forensic expert testified about what marks he found on the body during an autopsy. So, science classes are good. Math is important. We could have a big corporate breakup and then the economists would come in and testify and just some of the terms they throw around, you might need. Any English classes are always good because you are trying to make the lawyers make sense. We use their words, but sometimes we put dashes when we know they are going into a different thought or we try to put commas in the right place. Vocabulary is important.[59]

As many training programs offer distance-learning options, students able to access the Internet or get to a videoconference center can experience classroom training. Training programs vary in length, depending on whether a reporter chooses to become a stenotypist or a voice writer. It can take less than a year to become a voice writer, while the average length of study for a stenotypist is thirty-three months. NCRA-approved programs require students to be able to record a minimum of 225

A court reporter works with a stenograph during a trial. Court reporters undergo specialized training to learn how to operate the stenograph.

words per minute, so that they can meet the minimum standard for most jobs.

Gaining speed can be a challenge, but those who have been through a course advise would-be court reporters not to give up. Sherri Kostante, a recent graduate, says, "Nearly every budding reporter will 'hit the wall' at one speed or another and plateau for a long period of time. For me it was 120. I passed my 110 words per minute in April, but wasn't able to pass my 120 until September. That's a very long time to wait for 10 words a minute!"[60]

Most court reporters, however, face frustration and setbacks while building their skills. Says Janet Dransfield: "The first two years are periods of reward interspersed with short periods of terror. You're learning all the time, and everything is new—lots of new situations, terminology, and demands. But if the field is for you, you learn to love what you're doing despite the scary aspects."[61]

A court reporting student enrolled in an NCRA-approved program is able to gain confidence and experience through the program's internship component. Internships allow students to experience the various aspects of the job without the stress of being fully responsible. Dransfield explains why internships are crucial in helping new court reporters to feel better equipped in their first job: "When I went to school I didn't have one, and it made starting out terrifying. I really had no idea what to expect. Internships are a wonderful tool in helping a reporter decide what aspect of court reporting she likes, and in working out the first scary days of being in court or in a freelance atmosphere."[62]

Learning to Stenotype

Most court reporters record on a stenotype machine (also called a stenograph). A stenotype machine resembles a tiny typewriter. Each key prints a single symbol. As the court reporter presses multiple keys, the machine digitally records words, phrases, and syllables. Sounds also record onto a strip of paper as a backup. The notes are then translated into English using software designed specifically for court reporters. The court reporter prepares transcripts in printed or digital form, which she or he distributes to courts, lawyers, and the public upon request.

Increasingly, computer skills are vital to being a court reporter. In fact, the NCRA says that more than 90 percent of court reporters use computers in their work. Says Sue Williamson, "As we write, [the information] feeds into the computer and prints on continuous-feed paper. We still have a traditional paper tape, but we also have five or six backup systems on the computer."[63] Computers allow court reporters to offer more services, including condensed transcripts, which are several pages of testimony on one page.

When doing real-time translation, called communication access real-time translation (CART), court reporters link their stenotype machines to a computer. As they key in the symbols, the text is translated on the screen, giving others in the courtroom immediate access to the transcription. Says one reporter:

> I can connect my stenograph machine to my laptop, so the transcript comes up on the screen as I am writing. I can have a second laptop on the bench so the judge can have a screen in front of him. If an attorney brought a laptop into court, I could connect to his laptop, and he could read testimony in real time on his screen.[64]

After recording, court reporters edit their transcripts for correct grammar, for accurate identification of proper names and places, and to ensure that the record or testimony makes sense. At this point the reporter's own judgment comes into play, and he or she must be careful not to change the intended meaning of whoever was speaking. Says court reporter Jacqueline Timmons:

> You will find that not all witnesses speak in complete sentences, which makes it difficult to punctuate. If a witness pauses in his or her answer, it may not necessarily mean that a comma belongs in the space. The witness may just be thinking how to phrase the answer or may be ready to change thought altogether, in which case you need to place a dash.[65]

Alternative Method

A second method of reporting, used less frequently, is voice writing. In this method court reporters speak directly into a stenomask,

During a break in the proceedings, a judge discusses a trial's transcript with the court reporter. The transcript may include videotapes of court documents and exhibits, as shown here.

which is a handheld mask that contains a microphone with a device called a voice silencer, which absorbs the sound of their voice. As the reporter repeats the testimony into the recorder, the mask and silencer prevent the reporter from being heard. Voice writing allows for a more complete record than an audio record would. Not only is all testimony equally audible, but the recorder can also indicate gesture and emotional reactions during proceedings. Voice writers face the daunting challenge of quickly listening and speaking simultaneously. Another challenge is identifying speakers and describing peripheral activities that are happening in the room.

Huge Learning Curve

While schooling sets basic skills, real learning occurs on the job. One reality that quickly hits, says Timmons, is that taking dictation on the job differs significantly from class dictation, as people speak at different speeds: "It will vary all through the day, depending on who is speaking. The lawyer may be slow and the witness fast or vice versa."[66]

Until they build their experience and speed, reporters are not ready to report for the courts. To build both, new court reporters gain valuable experience recording depositions for attorneys or working as freelance reporters. Janet Konarski, a court reporter for twenty-five years, says, "An agency will start you off with easier

A *court reporter uses a stenograph to record the testimony of a witness.*
Achieving proficiency on the stenograph can take years.

projects, such as personal injury cases, that might only take an hour to do. As the court reporter gains experience and confidence, they will be given more challenging assignments."[67]

Achieving top speeds can take years, but court reporter Michelle Huskey-Smith says that daily practice is the key to improving:

> Try not to get distracted at times when you are frustrated at the speed at which you're progressing. As long as you know that you are making a serious effort to improve, then it shouldn't bother you. . . . I realized that continuous daily

dedication, a desire to succeed and a positive reflection on how well I had done up to that point were the only factors that I needed to progress.[68]

A court reporter's speed depends upon more than manual dexterity. Though they must be able to quickly set up their machines, there are some "cheats" that can help them to clean up their transcriptions later. Experienced reporters know this, and prepare for each job by customizing their computer dictionaries with parts of words, entire words, or terminology specific to the proceeding, program, or event. By adding these words beforehand to their online dictionaries, court reporters can record them with a single keystroke. But without a good dictionary, court reporters may have to spend many hours cleaning their transcripts. Kostante notes that after two months as a court reporter, she is still working on her dictionary: "It will probably take close to a year to get my dictionary in good shape. My writing isn't as 'clean' as I would like it to be. I have to spend way too much time editing right now."[69]

Reference books such as scientific dictionaries, medical dictionaries, and books of abbreviations and acronyms are invaluable tools, says Timmons: "If you cannot afford to keep your own library at first, your local library may have what you need."[70] She adds:

> Don't get discouraged if your first reporting assignment doesn't leave you with a warm, fuzzy feeling. I have been reporting for 13 years, and I still love it. That doesn't mean I haven't had some horrible assignments that have left me wanting to cry. But those unfavorable experiences didn't ruin it for the other assignments—those that have left me feeling I chose a very rewarding career.[71]

Certifications

Some states require court reporters to pass a state test to become certified court reporters (CCRs) or certified shorthand reporters (CSRs). To promote their skills, court reporters may choose to take the NCRA's registered professional reporter (RPR) exam. The test is difficult: There are one hundred multiple-choice questions that focus on four areas: reporting, transcript production, operating practices, and professional issues. Test takers have ninety minutes to complete this section of the exam, and must get a score of 70 percent to pass. Applicants also need to pass three sections of a skills test that evaluates dictation speed. Upon transcribing their notes from each test, reporters need an accuracy rate of 95 percent to pass. When they pass the entire test (the parts can be taken separately), reporters earn the designation registered professional reporter. The highest certification for speed plus written knowledge is the registered merit reporter (RMR). Most court reporters need five to ten years of experience to meet the RMR requirement of recording at 260 words per minute. The NCRA also offers testing for certified realtime reporter (CRR), certified broadcast captioner (CBC), certified CART provider (CCP), and registered diplomat reporter (RDR) designations.

Konarski notes that although the NCRA titles are not required for all reporting jobs, they help reporters to command better assignments and higher salaries:

The CRR tests accuracy, the RMR tests speed. If you have these certifications then you can get into the difficult and

Branching Out

Beyond working for the courts or other firms needing a recording of a legal proceeding, court reporters often provide captioning of live television programming for people who have hearing loss. Many reporters are able to significantly supplement their incomes by doing so, as their skill at quickly typing what they hear is in high demand. And that demand is growing, thanks to the Federal Telecommunications Act of 1996, which requires that all new television programming offer captioning by 2006, to benefit the approximately 100 million Americans who are elderly, learning English, or hard of hearing. When working on live captioning, court reporters are referred to as stenocaptioners.

A court reporter transcribes the closing argument of a defense attorney as the judge looks on. Most official court reporters work for one judge exclusively.

technical cases. In federal court they are now requiring reporters to be CRRs or obtain it within a year of being hired. A reporter with only the state certification, working forty hours a week, might make only $50,000 a year. A reporter with the CRR and RMR can make $100,000 a year.[72]

Salaried Reporters

Official court reporters are typically hired by and work exclusively for a judge. They are expected to have speed and expert knowledge of legal terminology and criminal and appellate procedures. As official reporters spend a lot of time with their judges, a good working relationship is critical, says court reporter Rhonda Menor: "It is essential that trust and respect flow both ways in an officialship. Without it, the relationship has no foundation and is destined for failure. Officials who do not respect their judges can't possibly experience total fulfillment in their jobs. Likewise, officials who lack respect from their judges work in constant frustration."[73]

Outside the courtroom, the salaried reporters are responsible for other duties, including fielding phone calls and conducting research. One court reporter describes her typical day:

> When we get ready for a hearing, sometimes in the morning, I'll look through the files. I get the caption of the case and the parties' names. If I am doing real time for that trial or if I think they'll want it typed up, I will input names into my dictionary. I will write them on my machine and then hi-light those words and input it into my dictionary so they are there when we do the real time. If I deal with the attorneys, I ask them ahead of time what exhibits they would like marked. I typically go through exhibits ahead of time, particularly if we are having an emotional trial. . . . I look at that so it doesn't bother me once we are in the middle of trial. I kind of just look through things ahead of time so I know what to expect.[74]

A downside of these salaried positions is that if a judge is not reappointed, the reporter may lose his or her job as well.

Freelance Reporters

According to the NCRA, only about 27 percent of court reporters in the United States actually work in full-time positions in the various courts. Instead, most reporters freelance, working with agencies that match them with assignments in exchange for a percentage of their per-page fee. Freelance reporters use their own equipment, including a stenotype machine, laptop computer, translation software, and printer. Leach explains why she prefers freelancing: "I like the variety of it. I'm in a different place all the time."[75] Church adds that she likes working out of her home office: "I can take a break and do a load of laundry or get dinner started and then get back to my transcripts. . . . On sunny days, I love to sit on the deck and work on my laptop."[76]

The disadvantage of being a freelance reporter is the uneven work flow: Some weeks might bring multiple assignments; other times, days will go by with no assignments. And there is the chance that assignments will be cancelled at the last minute, too late to arrange another assignment. Thus, freelance reporters are not guaranteed a consistent monthly income.

Freelancers have other worries as well: If they lose the ability to use their hands, they are unable to work—and they must pay for their own health care. These factors drive some reporters to look for full-time salaried positions. Menor explains her hasty retreat from freelancing:

> Oh, it wasn't that I didn't like freelancing; I downright hated it. I hated traveling. I hated not having a definite income I could depend on. I hated not having benefits—no paid vacations, no insurance and no retirement account. I hated paying my taxes quarterly. I hated lugging my equipment around everywhere I went. I hated the last-minute cancellations, and I hated working someplace different every day.[77]

Outlook

Its mental and physical demands make court reporting a stressful occupation. Physical problems include carpal tunnel syndrome and other repetitive motion disorders caused by frequent typing. If a court reporter ignores the pain instead of seeking a doctor's assistance, the disorders can cause long-term pain in the hands, wrists, neck, and shoulders, and quickly put an end to his or her career. But of the 25 percent who leave the profession between their first and second years, most cite stress as the major factor in their decision. Thirty percent of court reporters who leave become medical transcribers. Some take jobs as secretaries or assistants. Others move on to administrative and management positions, consulting, or teaching.

Rewarded for their aptitude and dependability, court reporters enjoy challenging careers. Reporters' earnings depend on their location, level of training and certification, areas of specialization, and the number of hours they work. Official court reporters earn a salary and a per-page fee for preparing transcripts and freelance reporters receive a per-page fee for transcripts and a flat fee for each assignment. According to the Bureau of Labor, in 2002, court reporters earned a median annual salary of $41,550.

Repetitive Stress Injuries

Because they use their hands in a way that requires making the same motions time after time, court reporters can suffer from repetitive stress injuries (RSIs). RSIs are conditions caused by repetitive motions that put pressure on nerves or soft tissue. Muscles, nerves, and tendons can become inflamed and painful. Court reporters often get RSIs from sitting in one place for hours at a time, often in postures that stress their muscles. Some court reporters find that areas of their bodies become tight or ache when they become stressed. These might include their lower backs, shoulders, necks, or forearms. Though these conditions can be temporary irritations, permanent damage can occur in the hands, wrists, elbows, neck, shoulders, and back if they are not addressed. To treat RSIs, court reporters may need to reduce the number of hours they work or take an extended break until the symptoms subside. Pausing to stretch and relax during assignments is a good idea, although not always possible. Aspirin, acetaminophen, ibuprofen, or other nonsteroidal anti-inflammatory drugs can be effective in treating inflammation and stiffness. To prevent such injuries, some court reporters wear supportive braces while they work.

The current shortage of court reporters translates to excellent job opportunities. Janene Thibault, co-owner of Metropolitan Court Reporters Inc. in Overland Park, Kansas, concurs that the short supply of court reporters cannot meet current demand: "With all the new positions available for court reporters, the void has widened, and that makes it harder for us to cover our clients' needs."[78] Konarski notes that court reporting is a particularly great career for those who want to work only part-time so they can pursue other interests: "There is no other job like it for flexibility, and the income is good."[79]

Chapter 5

Law Librarians

Law librarians are indispensable to the U.S. legal system, whether working in academic (university) libraries, government agency libraries, state public law libraries, court libraries, or private law firm libraries. Lawyers and paralegals depend upon librarians to help them to quickly find information. Says attorney John Scanlon: "Without the assistance of law librarians, I believe that many of us practicing attorneys would slog endlessly through tomes of case law and statute books in our search for material on point. The law librarian is the one reliable guide in leading lawyers and laymen to firm ground."[80]

Judges, likewise, might seek a librarian's assistance in locating previous court rulings. As U.S. Supreme Court Justice Sandra Day O'Connor notes, "In my work, a good library is essential. It enables me to learn the background and previous discussion of the various issues I am called upon to decide."[81]

A law librarian returns a volume of case law to the shelf. Lawyers and paralegals rely on law librarians to help them locate information relevant to their cases.

Thus, librarians bring considerable value to the practice of law. Connie Smith, head librarian at a private law firm, shares how she views her role:

> I am not a lawyer by training, but I am essential to the lawyers—and they know that. I think my judgment and my planning are respected. . . . We are constantly responding to variety of challenges, and we make contributions that go way beyond just finding relevant case law for associates' research assignments. Today's law library function is complex, sophisticated and very technology intensive.[82]

The American Association of Law Libraries (AALL) highlights a further benefit that law librarians provide—cost savings: "Recent studies show that it costs professional organizations, on average, three times more per person to obtain information from a library if an employee searches for it without help, than if a trained librarian assists with the search."[83]

Law librarians also serve as a valuable resource to the general public: Ordinary citizens often wander into university or court libraries after deciding to handle their own cases. With a law librarian's knowledge of available law-related materials, visitors can avoid hours of aimlessly searching through book stacks, periodicals, and online databases. Because of this skill, the AALL considers law librarians to be diplomats in a foreign land, guides who help information seekers to distill their information needs. After they help patrons to determine what they really need, law librarians are then able to direct them to the most appropriate sources and demonstrate how to use them. Law librarians routinely offer classes on how to search online legal databases.

Common Traits

Librarians, by nature, are organized individuals, an attribute that is called upon daily. Their tasks involve organizing not just materials and information, but people, projects, and procedures. For example, a librarian in a law school library might design a reservation system that guarantees students equal access to the library's study rooms, while a librarian in a busy law firm might devise a checkout system that ensures that attorneys promptly return materials.

Tools in Print

To assist lawyers, judges, and the general public, law librarians have access to a variety of printed sources. Some of the most popular sources include legal encyclopedias, statute and code books, legal journals, and case reports. Law encyclopedias list topics alphabetically. Code books organize statutes and codes passed by Congress or a state legislature by topic. Legal journals feature articles that highlight recent legal topics. Case report books highlight the facts of a case as well as the judgments made by the trial court and appellate court or Supreme Court. Until the information is printed as hardcover books, case information is published weekly as pamphlets called advance sheets.

Librarian Mary Whisner notes that law librarians share another trait—flexibility:

> In a given week, a reference librarian might work at the reference desk, do research for a partner or professor, serve on a committee, edit a newsletter, conduct a training session, and clear a printer jam. Meanwhile a technical services librarian might catalog some books, supervise the paraprofessional who is checking in serials, negotiate a contract with a bibliographic utility, serve on a university committee, and write a policy manual.[84]

Because librarians must accommodate numerous requests for help during their busy day, Whisner adds that librarians need to enjoy serving people in order to experience satisfaction in their job:

> If you like customer service and you enjoy coming up with ways to serve your organization better, you could have a long, happy life in the profession. On the other hand, if you do not like the idea of setting your project aside because Professor Procrastinator or Larry the Last Minute Litigator has a deadline, then you might find some parts of law librarianship vexing.[85]

Thus, being able to remain calm and polite is important, says librarian Jim Gernert, as "sometimes patrons can be fairly demanding in terms of the information that they expect you to provide."[86] Law librarians, however, cannot function as lawyers. Librarian Jean Callihan explains: "Law librarians must be careful not to cross the line from helping people with research to giving unlicensed legal advice."[87]

Educational Requirements

While it is not always necessary to have a law or library degree to get a job as a law librarian, libraries are increasingly requiring candidates to have a master's degree from an American Library Association–accredited library school. Currently, 85 percent of law librarians possess a Master of Library Science (MLS) degree. Librarians working in the reference areas of academic law libraries typically need a law degree as well, says Callihan, to best help law students: "It doesn't matter which degree you obtain first. Some people practice law first and bring a bit of real world experience with them. Others get their MLS first and then attend law school. This second path is probably the least stressful because you can enjoy the study of law without having to pass the bar exam."[88]

Law librarians know which resources to consult from among a law library's many volumes. Most librarians obtain a Master of Library Science degree as part of their training.

Gernert became a legal librarian after finishing law school. He believes his legal training allows him to more effectively help patrons:

> I really didn't have a clear-cut idea that I wanted to do this as a career, but I'd always enjoyed spending time in libraries, and had worked in libraries before going to law school. After I practiced law for a few years I realized that I wasn't comfortable with the adversarial mode of practicing law, and thought that working in the law library was a way that I could use my legal education in an environment that was more comfortable for me. I think that having a law degree helped with my analytical skills, along with increasing my knowledge of legal research tools. It also helps me to empathize with the sometimes stressful situations in which the patrons can find themselves.[89]

Callihan also practiced law before becoming a librarian at Cornell Law Library. She shares that the confrontational environment of litigation did not satisfy her desire to help people:

> The more time I spent as an attorney and the higher I moved up the career ladder, the less satisfying I found the hours spent at my job. I finally consulted with a career counselor, a financial planner (becoming a law librarian meant a substantial pay cut), and several librarians—law, public, special, and school—before returning to school for my MLS. At first I explored the possibility of working as a special librarian in a corporate setting. However, I came to realize that I had valuable legal research knowledge and skills that made law librarianship the logical choice.[90]

Many master's programs in library and information science can be completed in a year if a student attends school full-time. However, some programs can take two years to complete and may require a thesis and/or fieldwork. Many schools offer distance education instruction so students who do not live near the school can enroll in their programs. In addition, some schools offer dual programs that allow a student to simultaneously earn a law degree and library degree. Most of these programs take at least four years of study.

Library students who take advantage of library intern programs, says lawyer and law librarian Frances Brillantine, will not only be helped in their studies, but gain insight into which law library environment will most appeal to them: "Especially once you have enrolled in an MLS program, experience in a library will be of tremendous benefit to you and will help you to apply what you're learning in class to the 'real world.'"[91]

A Changing Job

Today's librarians cannot ignore changing technology as they go about their jobs. Not only do librarians use computers throughout the day for e-mail and correspondence, they use them to access a wide variety of information via online databases such as Westlaw, Lexis, and Dialog. These subscription-based databases provide information on cases, state and federal statutes, and other legal information. At times the sheer volume of material threatens to become overwhelming. Says Callihan, "Even as an information professional you may be overwhelmed by the information out there. You can't know everything, but you can learn to find quite a bit of it and how to evaluate the good information from the bad."[92]

Flexibility is also necessary because the technology that law librarians use every day is constantly evolving, says Smith:

> We have to stay current even as technology, systems, software and whole approaches to organizing legal information evolve constantly. We really can't plan out longer than about two years, because information management may move in directions we can't foresee today. This is also probably the greatest strain on law librarians. By nature, librarians are people who need and like order. We organize things. But the information management world is disorganized and chaotic; it frequently runs against our orderly grain. Today, a successful legal librarian must be flexible, adaptable and be "quick study." He or she really must be comfortable with technology, seeing it as a boon and not an annoyance. It's not a field for someone to consider simply because they love books.[93]

Keeping Up with Technology

During a presentation given at the Special Libraries Association (SLA) Annual Conference in 1998, information broker Susan Fingerman reminded attendees that staying completely current with technology is impossible. Fingerman offered a number of tips to help law librarians find information on the Internet. Following is an excerpt from her presentation, which was printed in the May 1999 issue of Information Outlook:

My first advice is to step back, take a deep breath, and think. Think about what you've done over the past years as an information professional. You know the techniques of research, of evaluating sources. You master numerous different interfaces, practice the art of the reference interview, and translate need into the knowledge of where to look for the information in the format required using the most cost-effective and timely methods. In short, you have developed and honed all the skills necessary for this now seemingly hopeless task.

And that is my second piece of advice—it IS a hopeless task. But that's okay. NO ONE is comprehensively keeping up with the Internet. The smart people aren't really trying. They are concentrating hardest on the information they need. Granted, as information professionals, we may need to keep up with, and even ahead of, more than most. We're concerned with, and expected to be informed about, the hardware, the software, the searching methods, the output options, the costs (cause WE know it ain't all free!), and of course the sites of reputable, authoritative, and current information. And the pace is dizzying compared to the good old days when DIALOG announced eight new databases a month, LEXIS-NEXIS rearranged its libraries only every six months to a year and DOW JONES added ten new publications a week.

A fairly new task law librarians might handle is managing in-house computer networks. Librarians working in law firms may be responsible for ensuring that lawyers in offices across the country are electronically connected and updated, with access to information that is not physically available in their local offices.

Private Law Librarians

Librarians employed by law firms and corporate legal departments are called private law librarians. In addition to managing information, private law librarians help to collect information on witnesses, monitor legislative and regulatory developments, and conduct research that supports the attorneys' cases. Kathie Sweeney, a library director, notes that in a typical week she might renew subscriptions to legal publications, evaluate new publications or services to see if they would fill a need not covered by other materials, and eliminate publications that no longer serve a need. She also maintains the firm's library database, which contains the library's records, routing lists, and online catalog. Sweeney also locates articles and other information, scans the news for articles that might interest her lawyers, and organizes training for attorneys, paralegals, and secretaries on searching online databases. She also spends time networking with other local and national librarians, attends professional meetings, and participates in activities with the AALL.

Library staffs in law firms are usually small. Often, one person has to handle all aspects of the operation. Sweeney shares some of the downsides to being in charge of all areas of a library: "I am a solo librarian. So when I am out of the office on vacation my work is not done by someone else while I am away. It is waiting for me when I return. I generally try to take vacation in the form of long weekends since being out longer causes a backlog that sometimes takes several weeks to catch up on."[94]

As most private law libraries are also physically small, library staffs face space constraints on the amount of printed information they can offer their lawyers. Thus, emerging technology, such as law books on CD-ROM, is a welcome alternative. Smith shares how technology dictates the way private librarians provide service:

> The library as a physical space is going away. While there always will be a repository for books (because research shows there are differences between how much someone will read and download from a computer screen versus how much they will read in a book), we really are pushing knowledge down to lawyers' desktops. Our role is about

Although law libraries like this one continue to house extensive print collections, most offer computer resources as well. Law librarians are adept at using all available resources.

managing knowledge—and managing the technology that manages knowledge. It's not about shelving books.[95]

Sweeney agrees: "I have seen the library become more computer work and less books. If a firm needs space, chances are the library gets downsized once again. That not only applies with space, but with staff also. Gone are the days of the impressive libraries that were once firms' showpieces."[96]

Academic Law Librarians

Physical space is less of a concern in a law school library, where legal librarians handle and shelve many books. According to a 1991 survey of more than 175 law schools accredited by the American Bar Association, the average law school library has more than three hundred thousand books in print and microform, employs eight professional staff members, and spends nearly $1.4 million each year. Thus, academic law librarians spend much of their time acquiring, cataloging, and maintaining their printed library collections.

Even so, technology is dictating change. Gernert, an electronic resources librarian at the University of Baltimore School of Law Library, notes that most law students, however, are more

A team of attorneys works with printed materials in preparation for a case. Most librarians direct their patrons to a mix of electronic and print resources.

comfortable using online resources: "I think that they've grown up searching for things on the Internet, and don't really appreciate the added value that books sometimes can bring to one's research."[97] Gernert notes that newer technology is not always better. He explains how printed matter is a better choice in some circumstances: "I really like to use a mix of books and online resources; for any sort of background reading I prefer books, and also for things where I may need to flip back and forth between sections, such as with statutes. With searching for cases, though, online is much quicker and easier."[98]

Other librarians agree. Says Lynn Fritsch: "Physical libraries still exist because many print materials are simply better than their electronic counterparts. You still need copies for research. And the art of highlighting and writing notes in the margins can't be replaced electronically."[99] David Ensign, a head law librarian and professor of law at the University of Louisville, adds:

People assume that there will be less and less need for libraries—that libraries will shrink in size and people will need less help and that online sources will supplant printed sources. . . . But what appears to be happening is that there's been a continuing increase in the publication of books and journals and loose-leaf services and things that are in print—and an increase in what's available online.[100]

It is the academic law librarian's role to help students to effectively navigate this burgeoning amount of information. As law school is already so challenging, students do not have the luxury of wasting time when searching for information. Gernert explains how he assists students:

I work at the reference desk two to three hours a day, answering patron questions related to legal research. I also keep track of the electronic resources, including renewing subscriptions, taking care of problems, and just answering

Volumes of case law compiled through the years can occupy hundreds of bookshelves, as this view of the interior of the University of San Francisco Law Library shows.

questions about them. Along with some of the other librarians, I also do training sessions on the databases and other resources for our students.[101]

As academic librarians spend many hours teaching others, they need good presentation skills.

Academic law librarians also assist professors and other university staff, lawyers who cannot find what they need in their firm libraries, and the general public. In the process, librarians do many different types of chores. For example, Brillantine, head of access services at Catholic University's Judge Kathryn J. DuFour Law Library in Washington, D.C., contributes content and design input for the Web site the library maintains. In addition, Brillantine creates promotional materials for the library. She also oversees the library's circulation department, interlibrary loan procedures, course reserves, and stacks maintenance, and provides backup assistance to the reference librarians. She also addresses patron concerns and supervises three full-time employees and twenty-five part-time student workers. Many libraries offer scholarship positions to library students. In her library, Brillantine supervises the students admitted into the three schol-

Academic law librarians help law students like this one conduct research and prepare for their difficult exams.

The Law Library of Congress

Established in 1800 as an in-house reference library for the use of the nation's lawmakers, the Law Library of Congress contains the world's largest collection of law books and other legal resources from the world (approximately 260 existing nations and dependencies as well as many former nations and colonies). The law library originally contained 2,011 volumes, 639 of which had been part of Thomas Jefferson's private library. In 1899 the law collection consisted of 103,000 volumes (including 15,000 duplicates), of which about 10,000 were in foreign languages. In 1989 its holdings surpassed 2 million volumes. Digital information is available via online databases.

The library's librarians provide research and legal information to Congress, the federal courts, executive branch agencies, and the general public. The library allows researchers who are eighteen years or older, with a valid photo identification (such as a driver's license or passport) and current address, to look through the library's collection.

High school students under age eighteen may use the library for a single day if their local public and university libraries are unable to provide the information they seek—and if they have identified that the material is available only at the Law Library of Congress. In addition, students must have a letter from their principal that describes their project. The final bar to entry is an interview with a reference librarian in the Law Library Reading Room. The librarian determines if the project requires the use of the library's collections.

arship positions it offers to library students as part of its graduate library preprofessional (GLP) program.

Government Librarians

Government librarians work in state, court, county, and bar association libraries. They interact with judges, public defenders, and prosecutors. The public often uses government libraries when looking for information on how to write a will or file for divorce. Some patrons visit because they want help with accessing online court records. Librarian Scott Stevens admits that the most enjoyable part of his job is interacting with people. He says he likes the fact that each day brings new challenges, as he never knows what patrons will need help in locating: "While the majority of people who come in look for material on divorce and custody, we're just as likely to get someone looking for laws on barking dogs or environmental laws because they think their property constitutes a 'wetland.'"[102]

On a typical day Stevens assists patrons in locating books, renting audiovisual equipment, and accessing online databases. He also spends a lot of time filing, an activity that never ends. Stevens explains, "There is an awful lot of material that is updated regularly, so there is constant filing of updates to that material."[103] In addition, he networks with other librarians, which helps him to know which libraries have materials that his library does not. This allows the libraries to share resources.

Outlook

According to a survey the AALL conducted of its members in 2003, general law librarians with two to five years of experience and a MLS earn an average of $40,666, or $54,059 if they have a JD and MLS. Reference librarians with a master's degree and two to five years of experience average $48,312, or $51,301 if they also have a law degree. Typically, law firms offer the highest salaries. The role of law librarian is challenging, satisfying, and always changing. Brillantine says it has been the perfect fit for her many interests:

> I decided to become a librarian while still in college because I enjoyed research and loved to read. My first two library jobs just happened to be in law libraries. The second one was in a public law library. I really enjoyed learning how to research statutes and cases and helping people. It was like a whole new world. I worked there my senior year and after only a few months I knew that I wanted to focus on law librarianship.[104]

Chapter 6

Mediators

Americans are increasingly willing to look to the courts to settle criminal and civil (noncriminal) disputes. Neighbors feuding over property lines and roommates bickering over unpaid bills, for example, believe that the courtroom is the only place they can get their issues resolved. The rush to court, however, is creating crowded court dockets, long delays, and lots of expenses. Fortunately, there is an alternative that not only offers faster results, but is much cheaper. It is a process called mediation.

Mediation is based on a principle called alternative (or appropriate) dispute resolution (ADR). ADR was first used in the United States in the late 1960s. It is based on the belief that solutions are possible with effective communication and negotiation, which is preferable to using adversarial processes such as courtroom litigation.

Those who practice mediation are called mediators (and sometimes conflict resolution specialists, facilitators, and labor relations specialists). Mediators meet with disputants in private settings to help them settle their legal problems outside the courtroom. Although similar to judges in that they control the proceedings, mediators do not make legal rulings. Rather, their job is to listen as the disputants state their case within a neutral environment, and then guide the parties in creating their own solution.

To be successful at this, mediators have to be great listeners; they must be able to identify the key issues that are fueling the conflict. Mediator Tara Fishler describes how she did this to resolve a situation in which two neighbors were at odds over a shared driveway: "You have to find out what the issues are for both sides. Is it that the car is parked too close to their house? Or that they always have to ask their neighbor to move their car so they can get out?"[105]

A team of mediators reviews documents to help resolve a dispute between two parties.

Once mediators have identified the issues, they then need the people skills to put the process into action. They also need sufficient powers of persuasion. Mediators use both to encourage the disputing parties to try to understand each other's perspective, and from there to craft a mutually agreeable solution. This creates a win/win situation for everyone involved. In Fishler's driveway example, she suggests that one solution might have been a parking schedule.

Training and Credentials

Although most mediators have a general understanding of the legal system, there is no particular need to have legal training. Though Fishler has a law degree and taps into that knowledge when needed, she thinks that there are two critical traits one needs to be an effective mediator: "Basically, you just need listening and communication skills."[106] Mediator Julie Denny notes several other attributes she thinks are critical: "A mediator is not like an assembly-line worker. You have to be able to think, have a high tolerance for conflict, and be able to see both sides of an issue."[107]

Many teachers, psychologists, pastors, lawyers, librarians, social workers, and human resource professionals work at least part-time as mediators. However, with the use of mediation growing, more universities now offer degree programs in conflict resolution that provide formal training for individuals who wish to be mediators. There are numerous other routes for gaining basic skills in mediation: Training sessions are offered by many local and national mediation organizations, independent companies, and nonprofit community mediation centers.

Often, community mediation centers charge the lowest fees for training in return for the students agreeing to volunteer their services at the center. This on-the-job training is an ideal way for students to hone their skills while gaining experience with a wide range of situations. Most people who complete training are then supervised through an apprenticeship. At first, graduates observe experienced mediators handling cases. They then begin to co-mediate cases with an experienced mediator, and finally move to mediating cases on their own.

Typically, mediators need twenty-five to forty hours of training to earn a certificate from their school. The certificate proves that they have completed a basic training. While some states

You Say Arbitrate, I Say Mediate

While people often interchange the terms "arbitrate" and "mediate" when referring to professionals who resolve disputes, the two roles are very different. In response to an article that appeared in the February 2004 issue of Inc. magazine, Raymond Patterson of the Civilian Complaint Review Board in New York City wrote to Inc. to explain why the two processes should not be confused. His letter appeared in the April 2004 issue:

The two terms should not be used synonymously. An arbitrator listens to both sides and eventually makes the final decision on how to resolve the dispute. A mediator, on the other hand, assists disputants in finding a resolution but does not make the decision for them. For ages, most people thought the only way to resolve disputes was to run to court. But litigation is usually the most severe and expensive way to resolve the issue. Arbitration was developed to avoid the pain of litigating, but it has grown so formal over the last century that many arbitrators identify the process they offer as a "trial." Mediation, which is more informal than either litigation or arbitration, is an incredibly powerful process not well-enough known in this country. It should not be confused with arbitration.

have independently established standards and training require-
ments, there are currently no national standards guiding the field.
Several prominent organizations, including the Association for
Conflict Resolution (ACR) and the New York State Dispute
Resolution Association, have formulated standards for certifica-
tion that will be utilized in the near future.

Differences in Mediation and the Courts

Mediators operate from the belief that when people become part
of creating a solution for themselves, they feel empowered and
more satisfied with the outcome. In contrast, courtroom judges
remove this option by making the decision for the disputants.
Mediators use emotion; judges rely on facts. Mediation sessions
and court sessions differ in other ways as well.

Mediation sessions, for example, are confidential and private;
only the disputants and the mediator involved know what is said
during them. This is the opposite of cases heard in court, which
become public record. Mediation also offers disputants the time

*The daughters of former president Richard Nixon take a break from a 2002
mediation hearing to resolve a dispute over terms of their father's will.*

they need to fully discuss their grievances. The overcrowded courts simply cannot extend this luxury. Because mediators approach their cases with empathy, the sessions work particularly well for people involved in emotionally charged disputes, such as employer/employee disputes, landlord/tenant disputes, victim/offender situations, school issues, animal complaints, divorce/separation disputes, and neighbor/neighbor disputes.

Fishler says mediation is more effective than litigation:

> I think any process that lets the parties be heard is better than a process where only their lawyers are heard. In a court case, people might be fighting over a dog. A mediator will say, "So, you really have strong feelings about this dog? Well, how much time do you spend maintaining the dog now?" The person might respond that they never walk it. A judge may not find that out.[108]

The Mediation Process

While mediation sessions are much less formal than a courtroom setting, they do contain structure. A session may start with the mediator expressing his or her hope that the participants will open themselves to discussion and to reaching a settlement. The parties are then invited to explain their part in the grievance and what they want to accomplish. In a divorce mediation, for example, a husband and wife may each express the desire to control the child visitation schedule, alimony payments, and how their assets are divided. After the mediator gets both sides to express their position and desired outcome, she or he then guides the parties in a joint discussion to see if there is any common ground. In some cases the mediator may meet with the parties individually (caucus) before leading the parties in joint negotiation. Caucuses may also be used during the session when either a party or the mediator feels the need to speak privately without the other party present. One party might, for instance, want the mediator's input on how to phrase a compromise.

If the parties are able to agree on a solution, the mediator may put the decision in writing, so that they have a formal agreement for themselves. Or, if the parties prefer, they may write up a contract that is legally binding. They might want this in case one of the disputants does not fulfill his or her part of the bargain, and the other wants to be able to prove this in court. However, if the parties cannot agree, the mediator can offer three options: The parties can meet again with the mediator at a later date after a cooling-off period; the parties can agree to binding arbitration in which a neutral person, typically an individual with a law background, acts as a judge, listening to both sides and then making a decision that in most cases is legally binding; or the parties can proceed with a court trial.

Court Blessings

Increasingly, judges recognize that mediation can produce an outcome in which everyone wins. Thus, many judges require that people seeking a decision by the court first attempt to resolve their disputes through mediation. Mediators may be appointed by the courts or chosen by the disputing parties. Judge James Lanuti offers his perspective on mediation: "It can be frustrating sometimes if you end up having to hear cases that really should have been resolved before they came to court. You see a lot of people who are almost self-destructive. I see that a lot in divorce cases. . . . And the saddest thing about it is to see the effect is has on children."[109]

As mediators charge much lower fees than lawyers do, people who cannot afford court costs often choose to mediate. However, mediation is not just for the poor; many individuals and companies of all economic strata are using mediation to avoid court. According to *Nolo's Encyclopedia of Everyday Law*, a half-day mediation of a personal injury claim (such as a car accident) might cost each party between five hundred and one thousand dollars. But if lawyers and the court get involved in the case, court fees could jump to fifty thousand dollars or more. In simpler neighbor/neighbor disputes, a full day of mediation, provided by a mediator on staff at a community mediation center, may cost each party only ten to fifty dollars. Even in cases in which large companies enter mediation to resolve a business dispute—a process that typically involves costs closer to ten thousand dollars—it is far less expensive than going to court, which could cost many tens of thousands of dollars.

Another benefit of mediation is that cases are resolved more quickly than if they were handled in court. Most mediation cases

A law professor coaches students engaged in a mock mediation hearing. Universities across the country offer degree programs in mediation.

are scheduled within weeks of a disputant requesting mediation, and are completed within weeks. Many cases are resolved in a single day or a single hour. In contrast, lawsuits can take months or years to resolve. Mediator Fran (Haug) Fletcher recalls a conflict she helped to resolve between an elderly man who was upset that leaves from his neighbor's trees were littering his yard. Fletcher discovered the real source of the man's anger after he demanded during the mediation session that the couple's sons rake his yard and they told him to "get a life":

> The man said, "I do have a life. And I have a wife. My wife is dying of cancer. I'm getting old, my wife is dying, and I can't control any of that. But I can control what happens in my yard." Do you think we were able to come to an agreement? You bet. The outcome was communication, empathy, and caring. The family now rakes their leaves and his. That, in a nutshell, shows the benefits of coming together. They each understood their own viewpoint, but not the other's viewpoint.[110]

Models of Mediation

While mediators develop their own styles, in general they follow one of three models. They might practice facilitative mediation,

transformative mediation, or evaluative mediation. Most mediators embrace the earliest form of mediation, the facilitative
model, which was first used in the United States in the 1960s.

In facilitative mediation, the mediator helps opposing parties
to reach a resolution that is agreeable to both of them. Typically,
the mediator asks the parties questions to uncover the issues that
need to be addressed, states that each disputant has the right to
his or her own point of view, and looks for common ground that
might motivate the disputants to discuss possible solutions. As
well, facilitative mediators strive to neutralize language as they
interact with participants. Fishler shares an example of how she
might do so: "If someone says, 'I hate your guts,' I'd say, 'So, you
seem to have strong feelings about her.'"[111]

A newer model, in use in the United States only since the
mid-1990s, is called transformative mediation. Transformative
mediators are less concerned with guiding the disputants toward
a solution to their current problem. Instead, transformative mediators are primarily interested in getting each party to understand
why the other has a different take on the problem, to understand
why they are reacting the way they do, and why they seek the
solution that they do. While the parties hopefully move toward
mutual understanding, transformative mediators feel it is appropriate if the parties do not find a compromise. Instead, they are
allowed to "agree to disagree."

As a transformative mediator, Denny describes what she
believes is her role:

> We believe that conflict is not a problem to be solved, but
> it's a breakdown in communication. This process is to facil-
> itate an improved human interaction. We believe when
> people are in conflict they're weak, frustrated, and self-
> involved. We try to move them to a state of strength so
> they're clear about what's important to them and thus more
> responsive to the needs of the other person. I'm trying to
> facilitate dialogue so they can get to the point of solving
> their own problems. They'll charge ahead on their own.[112]

Less often, mediators use the evaluative model. In this type of
mediation, the mediator listens to the disputing parties and

points out the weaknesses of each disputant's case. Ordinarily, he or she offers a prediction on what a judge or jury will decide if the case goes to court. Because this model involves providing a certain amount of legal advice, most evaluative mediators are attorneys.

The Issue of Neutrality

Except when using the evaluative model, mediators may find the most challenging task of their role is remaining neutral. No matter what their personal feelings might be, they must refrain from jumping in and guiding disputants toward the solution they think is best. Generally, their goal is to create a neutral environment that gives both parties the assurance that they are receiving equal treatment. Denny shares a tip one mediator uses: "I know a mediator who uses a metaphorical chest of drawers. He mentally puts his biases in a specific drawer and shuts it tight before he starts a mediation."[113] Denny's own mental checklist includes carefully monitoring the tone of her voice and being aware of any signals she might be sending out through her body language. She finds that nodding as a person speaks helps both parties to perceive her

A Full Career

People who gain skills in mediation can find themselves enjoying very satisfying careers. Michael Dickstein, a San Francisco–based mediator, arbitrator, and attorney, is a perfect example.

Not only is Dickstein the cochair of the Workplace Section of the Association for Conflict Resolution, he is on the ADR panels of numerous federal and state courts. During his career Dickstein has mediated numerous cases to successful settlements, including disputes involving employment, commercial, discrimination, contract, real estate, personal injury, malpractice, class action, and defamation issues. Dickstein has also worked internationally, facilitating contract negotiations between Canada's theater actors and major theater owners, and teaches courses on mediation and negotiation around the world.

A mediation expert poses next to a statue of the scales of justice. As mediation becomes a popular alternative to legal proceedings, the outlook for a career in the field is very promising.

as supportive, nonjudgmental, and interested in what they have to say. When she speaks, Denny adds, she chooses her words carefully: "One of the best ways to avoid the appearance of bias is to use the parties' own words in your interventions."[114]

Mediation in the Workplace

Whatever model they use, mediators are increasingly being called upon to help resolve workplace disputes. This is because many companies now find themselves being sued by employees who are upset. Many of these employee lawsuits involve issues of race, gender, age, handicap, and sexual orientation. Mediators can help employers and employees to try to solve their issues outside of court. Denny recalls a session she mediated between a supervisor and employee. The supervisor suspended the employee for two weeks for an on-the-job infraction. The employee wanted the suspension lifted. Using the transformative model, Denny achieved positive results for the employee: "At the end of the session she stood up and said, 'So this is mediation. I'm going to tell my friends.' She didn't get what she wanted, but she was really happy because she got her boss to listen to her. And back on the job he's going to treat her differently because now he understands how she feels."[115] Many companies also offer their employees training in conflict resolution, which gives them the tools to quickly settle conflicts.

Branching Out

Often, it is a freelance mediator who has designed that company training. Some mediators prefer to educate people on the benefits of ADR rather than handling the cases of those seeking to resolve actual problems. Others make a living by acting as trainers, introducing the concepts of ADR to groups of people or training other mediators. Here they have the chance to teach by conducting workshops, seminars, retreats, and conference sessions.

Fishler, for example, partners with schools, clubs, and companies. In schools, she trains students, teachers, parents, and administrators, as well as employees and supervisors, of all ages to be better listeners. The students also learn how to ask good questions that lead to conversation. While Fishler makes a living in introducing students to ADR, she is even more satisfied with the life tools she is helping the students to develop. "The students," she says, "might go home and be able to talk to their parents better."[116]

Similarly, Fletcher has conducted more than twenty-two hundred hours of training and coaching for state and community mediators, and county and town police departments. Another way mediators might supplement their incomes is by creating training programs and materials for companies who want to add ADR training modules to their employee training programs. Fletcher has helped to design and conduct training in collaborative problem-solving techniques for school administrators and teachers.

As most mediators do not work directly for a court system, and instead function as independent contractors, they are hired on an as-needed basis. This gives them freedom to pursue projects with a variety of clients. Because of this, most mediators must spend a lot of time marketing their skills to build their businesses. While they can eventually count on referrals from judges, to do so they must first become known in their local court system.

To find clients in their local communities, mediators often present free lectures to local organizations on the positive benefits of mediation. Mediators also look for appropriate places to distribute their promotional materials, as well as opportunities to appear in the newspaper, on radio shows, and on local TV and cable news programming. Says Denny, "If you really want to do this you have to commit to it. You have to hustle and market yourself."[117]

To build their name recognition beyond their local area, mediators often participate in national resolution associations such as the ACR, write articles for online mediation sites, and pay to list their name on the numerous mediator directories listed in print and on the Internet. Says Denny, "I get calls all the time from people seeing my articles. The Web is a great way to advertise."[118]

Outlook

According to the Princeton Review, there are currently more than six thousand mediators working in the United States. Most are self-employed. Most mediators do not start off working forty hours a week, and need to supplement their incomes while they build a reputation. However, mediators typically do not put in more than forty hours a week. With five years of experience, mediators make an average of $53,010; with ten to fifteen years of experience they might make more than $145,000. Most self-employed mediators charge hourly rates of seventy to two hundred dollars an hour, depending on their experience and the complexity of the mediation. With the increase in awareness and acceptance of mediation as an efficient method of solving conflicts, more and more people are being trained and utilizing this process. Thus, the field of mediation is expected to continue to grow.

Training Versus Experience

Many mediators choose to specialize in one area of mediation, such as family mediation or divorce and custody mediation. While most states still do not require private mediators to have certification, those who are certified have completed at least forty hours of basic mediation training. In addition, mediators who specialize tend to go on to take additional training courses in their specialty areas. Family mediators, for example, may have completed training to address parent/teenager issues, general family issues, adult guardianship, or family business. Similarly, mediators who specialize in divorce and custody mediation typically seek training in parenting arrangements, property division, emotional issues, conflict management, and financial management. As in any career field, mediators must then use their training to become competent in those areas. Training is important, but experience is the key to on-the-job success.

Fishler shares why she believes mediation is a satisfying career: "Mediation is something I totally believe in. It offers a simple, convenient method for disputants to come together in a neutral environment. We're not a society that says, 'You got a problem? Go talk to someone,' We either call an attorney and say, 'Fix it!' or call 911 and ask the cops to make it go away."[119]

Notes

Introduction: A Society Ruled by Law

1. David S. Mullally, *Order in the Court: A Writer's Guide to the Legal System*. Cincinnati, OH: Writer's Digest Books, 2000, p. 1.
2. Stephen Reinhardt, speech to the Beverly Hills Bar Association, June 4, 1996, Court TV Online. www.courttv. com/archive/legaldocs/misc/reinhardt.html.

Chapter 1: Paralegals

3. Quoted in Adam Kramer, "Paralegal Field Found One of Most Rapidly Growing," *Business Review*, April 18, 2003. http://albany.bizjournals.com/albany/stories/2003/04/21/focus7.html.
4. Steve Albrecht, *The Paralegal's Desk Reference*. New York: Prentice-Hall, 1993, p. xi.
5. Albrecht, *Paralegal's Desk Reference*, pp. 17–18.
6. Quoted in Blythe Camenson, *Careers for Legal Eagles & Other Law-and-Order Types*. Chicago: VGM Career Horizons, 1998, p. 63.
7. Nancy Slaughter, telephone interview with author, March 2004.
8. American Association for Paralegal Education, "Introduction: History and Diversity of Paralegal Education," *A Guide to Quality Paralegal Education*, 2003. www.aafpe. org/intro.html.
9. ParalegalGateway.com, "Degree vs. Certificate," chat center transcript, March 13, 2002. www.paralegalgateway. com/chat1.html.
10. Quoted in Camenson, *Careers for Legal Eagles & Other Law-and-Order Types*, pp. 244–245.
11. Slaughter, telephone interview.
12. Chere B. Estrin, *Paralegal Career Guide*, 2nd ed. New York: Wiley Law 1996, p. 58.

13. Albrecht, *Paralegal's Desk Reference*, p. 99.

14. Slaughter, telephone interview.

15. Quoted in Albrecht, *Paralegal's Desk Reference*, p. 90.

16. Estrin, *Paralegal Career Guide*, p. 57.

17. Quoted in Camenson, *Careers for Legal Eagles & Other Law-and-Order Types*, p. 256.

18. Marcy Jankovich, e-mail correspondence with author, April 2004.

19. American Association for Paralegal Education, "Introduction: History and Diversity of Paralegal Education."

20. Slaughter, telephone interview.

21. Brad J. Baber, "Secrets of Management Unveiled," *Legal Assistant Today*, March/April 2003. www.legalassistant today.com/issue_archive/feature_ma03.htm.

22. Estrin, *Paralegal Career Guide*, p. 193.

23. Stacey Hunt and Veronica DeCoster, "Branching Out on Your Own?" *Legal Assistant Today*, March/April 2002. www.legalassistanttoday.com/profession/branchingout.htm.

24. Marcy Jankovich, telephone interview with author, April 2004.

25. Jankovich, e-mail correspondence.

26. Jankovich, e-mail correspondence.

27. Quoted in Kramer, "Paralegal Field Found One of Most Rapidly Growing."

28. Jankovich, telephone interview.

Chapter 2: Lawyers

29. American Bar Association, "Preparation for Legal Education," www.abanet.org/legaled/prelaw/prep.html.

30. StudentMarket.com, "LSAT: About the Law School Aptitude Test," www.studentmarket.com/studentmarket/aboutlsat.html.

31. Marisa Schultz, "Law Grad's Suit Targets State Bar," *Detroit News*, May 5, 2003. www.detnews.com/2003/metro/0305/05/e01-155079.htm.

32. Joel Wattenbarger, telephone interview with author, March 2003.

33. Slaughter, telephone interview.

34. Gary Munneke, "The Truth About Jobs for J.D.s," American Bar Association, 2002. www.abanet.org/lsd/stu lawyer/sep02/thetruth.html.

35. Phil J. Shuey, "Finding a Life While Practicing Law," American Bar Association, www.abanet.org/genpractice/ lawyer/complete/may99shuey.html.

36. Quoted in Camenson, *Careers for Legal Eagles & Other Law-and-Order Types*, p. 11.

37. Quoted in Camenson, *Careers for Legal Eagles & Other Law-and-Order Types*, p. 12.

38. Christen Civiletto Carey, *Full Disclosure: The New Lawyer's Must-Read Career Guide*, 2nd ed. New York: ALM, 2001, pp. 157–158.

39. Donna Gerson, "Your Manners Are as Important as Your Skills and Experience," American Bar Association, 2001. www.abanet.org/lsd/stulawyer/dec01/jobs.html.

40. Carey, *Full Disclosure*, p. 143.

41. Carey, *Full Disclosure*, p. 159.

42. Reinhardt, speech to the Beverly Hills Bar Association.

43. Munneke, "The Truth About Jobs for J.D.s."

Chapter 3: Judges

44. Quoted in Camenson, *Careers for Legal Eagles & Other Law-and-Order Types*, p. 37.

45. Quoted in Brian Cookson, "Balance on the Bench," *Business Journal*, March 24, 2000. kansascity.bizjournals.com/ kansascity/stories/2000/03/27/focus1.html.

46. American Bar Association, "Richard Brown," ABA Career Counsel: Your Career Counsel on the Web, www.abanet. org/careercounsel/profile/judges/ brownr.html.

47. Mullally, *Order in the Court*, p. 28.

48. Judy Sheindlin, *Don't Pee on My Leg and Tell Me It's Rain-*

ing: America's Toughest Family Court Judge Speaks Out. New York: HarperCollins, 1996, p. 64.

49. Quoted in Camenson, *Careers for Legal Eagles & Other Law-and-Order Types*, p. 22.

50. Mullally, *Order in the Court*, p. 162.

51. Sheindlin, *Don't Pee on My Leg and Tell Me It's Raining*, p. 40.

52. Reinhardt, speech to the Beverly Hills Bar Association.

53. Sheindlin, *Don't Pee on My Leg and Tell Me It's Raining*, p. 40.

54. Quoted in Cookson, "Balance on the Bench."

Chapter 4: Court Reporters

55. Quoted in Pam Derringer, "Shortage of Court Reporters: The Writing Is on the Wall," *Boston Business Journal*, June 14, 2002. boston.bizjournals.com/boston/stories/2002/06/17/focus9.html.

56. Connie Church, "A Perfect Fit," *JCR Online*, July/August 2001. www.ncraonline.org/MembersOnly/jcr/0107/0107_perfect.htm.

57. Quoted in Dixie Yonkers, "On the Record," *Business Review*, April 20, 2001. http://albany.bizjournals.com/albany/stories/2001/04/23/focus1.html.

58. Church, "A Perfect Fit."

59. Quoted in Iowa Public Television, "Occupations: Court Reporter #1188," School to Careers, www.careers.iptv.org/people_detail.cfm?pplID=409#.

60. Sherri Kostante, e-mail correspondence with author, May 2004.

61. Janet Dransfield, e-mail correspondence with author, April 2004.

62. Dransfield, e-mail correspondence.

63. Quoted in Lisa Waterman Gray, "Court Reporters Have More Options than Transcribing Legal Proceedings," *Business Journal*, January 30, 2004. http://kansascity.bizjournals.com/kansascity/stories/2004/02/02/focus4.html.

64. Quoted in Mullally, *Order in the Court*, p. 40.

65. Jacqueline Timmons, "How to Make a Smooth Transition from Student to Reporter," NCRA Student Center, www.ncraonline.org/students/features/newjob.shtml.

66. Timmons, "How to Make a Smooth Transition from Student to Reporter."

67. Janet Konarski, telephone interview with author, April 2004.

68. Michelle Huskey-Smith, "A Long Road Traveled: From Student to Reporter," *JCR Online*, April 2001. www.ncra online.org/MembersOnly/jcr/014/0104_road.htm.

69. Kostante, e-mail correspondence.

70. Timmons, "How to Make a Smooth Transition from Student to Reporter."

71. Timmons, "How to Make a Smooth Transition from Student to Reporter."

72. Konarski, telephone interview.

73. Rhonda Menor, "Finding My Niche: Working as an Official Reporter," *JCR Online*, May 2001. www.ncraonline.org/MembersOnly/jcr/0105/0105_menor.htm.

74. Iowa Public Television, "Occupations: Court Reporter #1188."

75. Quoted in Yonkers, "On the Record."

76. Church, "A Perfect Fit."

77. Menor, "Finding My Niche."

78. Quoted in Gray, "Court Reporters Have More Options than Transcribing Legal Proceedings."

79. Konarski, telephone interview.

Chapter 5: Law Librarians

80. Quoted in American Association of Law Libraries, *Finding Your Way in the Information Age: The Many Roles of Law Librarians*, pamphlet.

81. Quoted in American Association of Law Libraries, *Finding Your Way in the Information Age*.

82. Quoted in NewYorkLawyer.com, "Alternative Careers," August 6, 2002. www.nylawyer.com/careers/02/080602.html.

83. American Association of Law Libraries, *Finding Your Way in the Information Age*.

84. Mary Whisner, "Choosing Law Librarianship: Thoughts for People Contemplating a Career Move," Law Library Resource Exchange, August 2, 1999. www.llrx.com/features/librarian.htm.

85. Whisner, "Choosing Law Librarianship."

86. Jim Gernert, e-mail correspondence with author, May 2004.

87. Jean Callihan, e-mail correspondence with author, May 2004.

88. Callihan, e-mail correspondence.

89. Gernert, e-mail correspondence.

90. Callihan, e-mail correspondence.

91. Frances Brillantine, e-mail correspondence with author, May 2004.

92. Callihan, e-mail correspondence.

93. Quoted in NewYorkLawyer.com, "Alternative Careers."

94. Kathie Sweeney, e-mail correspondence with author, May 2004.

95. Quoted in NewYorkLawyer.com, "Alternative Careers."

96. Sweeney, e-mail correspondence.

97. Gernert, e-mail correspondence.

98. Gernert, e-mail correspondence.

99. Quoted in Linda Romine, "Legal Librarians' Duties Evolve as Tech Highway Paves New Roads in Legal Documentation," *Business First*, April 6, 2002. http://louisville.bizjournals.com/louisville/stories/2002/04/29/focus3.html.

100. Quoted in Romine, "Legal Librarians' Duties Evolve as Tech Highway Paves New Roads in Legal Documentation."

101. Gernert, e-mail correspondence.

102. Scott Stevens, e-mail correspondence with author, May 2004.

103. Stevens, e-mail correspondence.

104. Brillantine, e-mail correspondence.

Chapter 6: Mediators

105. Tara Fishler, telephone interview with author, May 2004.

106. Fishler, telephone interview.

107. Julie Denny, telephone interview with author, May 2004.

108. Fishler, telephone interview.

109. Quoted in Camenson, *Careers for Legal Eagles & Other Law-and-Order Types*, p. 35.

110. Fran (Haug) Fletcher, interview with author, October 2000.

111. Fishler, telephone interview.

112. Denny, telephone interview.

113. Denny, telephone interview.

114. Denny, telephone interview.

115. Denny, telephone interview.

116. Fishler, telephone interview.

117. Denny, telephone interview.

118. Denny, telephone interview.

119. Fishler, telephone interview.

Organizations to Contact

American Arbitration Association
335 Madison Ave., Floor 10
New York, NY 10017-4605
(212) 716-5800
www.adr.org

This organization provides information about all forms of dispute prevention and resolution including mediation, arbitration, fact-finding, partnering, dispute review boards, and other related alternative dispute resolution processes.

American Association for Paralegal Education
407 Wekiva Springs Rd., Suite 241
Longwood, FL 32779
(407) 834-6688
www.aafpe.org

This national organization serves institutions that offer paralegal education programs.

American Association of Law Libraries
53 W. Jackson, Suite 940
Chicago, IL 60604
(312) 939-4764
www.aallnet.org

This organization exists to promote and enhance the value of law libraries to the public, the legal community and the world; to foster the profession; and to provide leadership in the field of legal information. The association represents law librarians and related professionals affiliated with a wide range of institutions: law firms, law schools, corporate legal departments, courts, and local, state, and federal government agencies.

American Bar Association (ABA)
740 15th St. NW
Washington, DC 20005-1019

(202) 662-1000

www.abanet.org

The ABA provides law school accreditation, continuing legal education, information about the law, programs to assist lawyers and judges in their work, and initiatives to improve the legal system for the public.

American Judges Association (AJA)

c/o National Center for State Courts

300 Newport Ave.

Williamsburg, VA 23185

(757) 259-1841

www.aja.ncsc.dni.us

The purposes of the AJA are to improve the effective and impartial administration of justice, enhance the independence and status of the judiciary, provide for continuing education of its members, and promote the interchange of ideas of a judicial nature among judges, court organizations, and the public.

Association for Conflict Resolution

1015 18th St. NW, Suite 1150

Washington, DC 20036

(202) 464-9700

www.acrnet.org

This organization is dedicated to enhancing the practice and public understanding of conflict resolution.

Federal Bar Association

2215 M St. NW

Washington, DC 20037

(202) 785-1614

www.fedbar.org

This professional organization, serving private and government lawyers and judges involved in federal practice, has been in existence for more than eighty years.

National Association of Legal Assistants (NALA)

1516 S. Boston, Suite 200
Tulsa, OK 74119
(918) 587-6828
www.nala.org

NALA is the leading professional association for legal assistants and paralegals, providing continuing education and professional development programs. NALA is composed of more than eighteen thousand paralegals, through individual members and through its ninety state and local affiliated associations.

National Court Reporters Association (NCRA)

8224 Old Courthouse Rd.
Vienna, Virginia 22182-3808
(800) 272-6272
www.ncraonline.org

NCRA is internationally recognized as the leading organization for court reporters. Through its large, active, and involved membership, the association has substantial impact on legislative issues and the global marketplace.

National Judicial College

Judicial College Building/MS 358
University of Nevada, Reno
Reno, NV 89557
(800) 255-8343
www.judges.org

This is the nation's leading judicial education and training institution.

For Further Reading

Books

Stephen Elias and Susan Levinkind, *Legal Research: How to Find and Understand the Law*, 11th ed. Berkeley, CA: Nolo Press, 2003. Provides information on using law libraries, conducting searches online, and other legal research methods.

Shae Irving, Kathleen Michon, and Beth McKenna, eds., *Nolo's Encyclopedia of Everyday Law*, 4th ed. Berkeley, CA: Nolo Press, 2002. A comprehensive desk reference for ordinary people seeking information on various aspects of the law. Sample chapters cover criminal law and procedure, courts and mediation, small business issues, and more.

Peter Lovenheim and Lisa Guerin, *Mediate, Don't Litigate.* Berkeley, CA: Nolo Press, 2004. Explains various aspects of using mediation to get what you want.

Kimm Alayne Walton, *What Law School Doesn't Teach You . . . But You Really Need to Know.* Orlando, FL: Harcourt Legal & Professional, 2000. Useful book full of tips including getting off on the right foot, smart researching, handling mistakes, and being your own career coach.

Web Sites

Find Articles, LookSmart.com (www.findarticles.com). A free full-text article search service with a database of more than three hundred reputable journals and magazines, searchable by keyword, subject, or name.

FindLaw (www.findlaw.com). Find cases, codes, forms, lawyer listings, dictionaries, consultants, organizations, and more.

LawInfo.com (www.lawinfo.com). Law information for the public and professionals.

Law Library Resource Xchange (www.llrx.com). An excellent source for top-notch research advice.

Mediate.com (www.mediate.com). Find information on mediation and mediators.

Researching Companies Online, LearnWebSkills.com (www.learn webskills.com/company/index.html). Free tutorial teaches how to find company and industry information on the Web.

The VirtualChase (www.virtualchase.com). Excellent research strategies, guides, articles, and resources for the Internet researcher, provided by librarian Genie Tyburski.

Works Consulted

Books

Steve Albrecht, *The Paralegal's Desk Reference*. New York: Prentice-Hall, 1993. This book shares information on interviewing techniques, reading police reports, and building relationships with other law professionals.

Blythe Camenson, *Careers for Legal Eagles & Other Law-and-Order Types*. Chicago: VGM Career Horizons, 1998. Includes long quotes from professionals working in various law careers.

Christen Civiletto Carey, *Full Disclosure: The New Lawyer's Must-Read Career Guide*, 2nd ed. New York: ALM, 2001. A lawyer herself, Carey shares how to negotiate a successful experience, from tips on figuring which law environment is best to building relationships that propel a law career forward.

Chere B. Estrin, *Paralegal Career Guide*. 2nd ed. New York: Wiley Law, 1996. A comprehensive guide on career advancement, including tips on résumés, interviewing, and opening a freelance business.

David S. Mullally, *Order in the Court: A Writer's Guide to the Legal System*. Cincinnati, OH: Writer's Digest Books, 2000. An excellent behind-the-scenes look at every aspect of the legal system.

Judy Sheindlin, *Don't Pee on My Leg and Tell Me It's Raining: America's Toughest Family Court Judge Speaks Out*. New York: HarperCollins, 1996. Using actual courtroom cases, Sheindlin shares her views on the shortcomings of the American legal system.

Ralph Warner, *The Independent Paralegal's Handbook*. Berkeley, CA: Nolo Press, 1996. A comprehensive guide on setting up a freelance paralegal business.

Periodical

American Association of Law Libraries, *Finding Your Way in the Information Age: The Many Roles of Law Librarians*, pamphlet.

Internet Sources

American Association for Paralegal Education, "Introduction: History and Diversity of Paralegal Education," *A Guide to Quality Paralegal Education*, 2003. www.aafpe.org/intro.html.

American Bar Association, "Preparation for Legal Education," www.abanet.org/legaled/prelaw/prep.html.

————, "Richard Brown," ABA Career Counsel: Your Career Partner on the Web, www.abanet.org/careercounsel/profile/judges/brownr.html.

Brad J. Baber, "Secrets of Management Unveiled," *Legal Assistant Today*, March/April 2003. www.legalassistanttoday.com/issue_archive/feature_ma03.htm.

Regina Chepalis, "Ten Things Every Paralegal Must Know About Electronic Evidence," *Facts & Findings*, May 2001. www.nala.org/May01TenThings.pdf.

Connie Church, "A Perfect Fit," *JCR Online*, July/August 2001. www.ncraonline.org/MembersOnly/jcr/0107/0107_perfect.htm.

Brian Cookson, "Balance on the Bench," *Business Journal*, March 24, 2000. kansascity.bizjournals.com/kansascity/stories/2000/03/27/focus1.html.

Pam Derringer, "Shortage of Court Reporters: The Writing Is on the Wall," *Boston Business Journal*, June 14, 2002. boston.bizjournals.com/boston/stories/2002/06/17/focus9.html.

District Attorney's Office of Los Angeles County, http://da.co.la.ca.us/.

Susan Fingerman, "Faster Than a Speeding Bullet—or, How to Keep Up with the Internet," *Information Outlook*, May 1999. www.findarticles.com/p/articles/mi_mOFWE/is_5_3/ai_55015339.

Donna Gerson, "Your Manners Are as Important as Your Skills and Experience," American Bar Association, 2001. www.abanet.org/lsd/stulawyer/dec01/jobs.html.

Lisa Waterman Gray, "Court Reporters Have More Options than Transcribing Legal Proceedings," *Business Journal*, January 30, 2004. http://kansascity.bizjournals.com/kansascity/stories/2004/02/02/focus4.html.

Stacey Hunt and Veronica DeCoster, "Branching Out on Your Own?" *Legal Assistant Today*, March/April 2002. www.legal assistanttoday.com/profession/branchingout.htm.

Michelle Huskey-Smith, "A Long Road Traveled: From Student to Reporter," *JCR Online*, April 2001. www.ncraonline. org/MembersOnly/jcr/014/0104_road.htm.

Iowa Public Television, "Occupations: Court Reporter #1188," School to Careers, www.careers.iptv.org/people_detail.cfm? pplID=409#.

Adam Kramer, "Paralegal Field Found One of Most Rapidly Growing," *Business Review*, April 18, 2003. http://albany.biz journals.com/albany/stories/2003/04/21/focus7.html.

Rhonda Menor, "Finding My Niche: Working as an Official Reporter," *JCR Online*, May 2001. www.ncraonline.org/Members Only/jcr/0105/0105_menor.htm.

Gary Munneke, "The Truth About Jobs for J.D.s," American Bar Association, 2002. www.abanet.org/lsd/stulawyer/sep02/the truth.html.

NewYorkLawyer.com, "Alternative Careers," August 6, 2002. www. nylawyer.com/careers/02/080602.html.

ParalegalGateway.com, "Degree vs. Certificate," chat center transcript, March 13, 2002. www.paralegalgateway.com/chat 1.html.

Raymond Patterson, letter to the editor, *Inc.*, February 2004. www.inc.com/magzine/20040401/mail.html.

Stephen Reinhardt, speech to the Beverly Hills Bar Association, June 4, 1996, Court TV Online. www.courttv.com/archive/ legaldocs/misc/reinhardt.html.

Linda Romine, "Legal Librarians' Duties Evolve as Tech Highway Paves New Roads in Legal Documentation," *Business First*, April 6, 2002. http://louisville.bizjournals.com/louisville/ stories/2002/04/29/focus3.html.

Marisa Schultz, "Law Grad's Suit Targets State Bar," *Detroit News*, May 5, 2003. www.detnews.com/2003/metro/0305/ 05/e01-155079.htm.

Phil J. Shuey, "Finding a Life While Practicing Law," American Bar Association, www.abanet.org/genpractice/lawyer/complete/may 99shuey.html.

StudentMarket.com, "LSAT: About the Law School Aptitude Test," www.studentmarket.com/studentmarket/aboutlsat.html.

Charlotte Thomas, "Snapshot of a Paralegal," Peterson's Career Education, www.petersons.com/careered/snapshot.html.

Jacqueline Timmons, "How to Make a Smooth Transition from Student to Reporter," NCRA Student Center, www.ncraonline. org/students/features/newjob.shtml.

Dixie Yonkers, "On the Record," *Business Review*, April 20, 2001. http://albany.bizjournals.com/albany/stories/2001/04/23/focus1. html.

Mary Whisner, "Choosing Law Librarianship: Thoughts for People Contemplating a Career Move," Law Library Resource Exchange, August 2, 1999. www.llrx.com/features/librarian.htm.

Index

Picture Credits

About the Author

Sheri Bell-Rehwoldt is the author of *Art*, another title in Lucent's Careers for the Twenty-First Century series. An award-winning freelance writer, she has written numerous articles on the arts, health, human resources, and interesting people for Web sites and national, regional, and trade publications, including *American Profile*, *Family Circle*, *HR Innovator*, and *Ladies Home Journal*. She also writes and edits for business and non-profit clients.